08/06

Beverly Cleary

WHO WROTE THAT?

Beverly Cleary

Jennifer Peltak

Foreword by
Kyle Zimmer

CHELSEA HOUSE
P U B L I S H E R S
A Haights Cross Communications Company®
Philadelphia

CHELSEA HOUSE PUBLISHERS

VP, NEW PRODUCT DEVELOPMENT Sally Cheney
DIRECTOR OF PRODUCTION Kim Shinners
CREATIVE MANAGER Takeshi Takahashi
MANUFACTURING MANAGER Diann Grasse

STAFF FOR BEVERLY CLEARY

EXECUTIVE EDITOR Matt Uhler
EDITORIAL ASSISTANT Sarah Sharpless
PRODUCTION EDITOR Noelle Nardone
PHOTO EDITOR Sarah Bloom
SERIES DESIGNER Keith Trego
LAYOUT 21st Century Publishing and Communications, Inc.

http://www.chelseahouse.com

A Haights Cross Communications ✈ Company ®

First Printing

1 3 5 7 9 8 6 4 2

Library of Congress Cataloging-in-Publication Data

Peltak, Jennifer.
  Beverly Cleary/Jennifer Peltak.
    p. cm.—(Who wrote that?)
  ISBN 0-7910-8231-8 (alk. paper)
  1. Cleary, Beverly—Juvenile literature. 2. Authors, American—20th century—
Biography—Juvenile literature. 3. Children's stories—Authorship—Juvenile
literature. I. Title. II. Series.
PS3553.L3914Z86 2004
813'.54—dc22

                                                    2004022975

All links and Web addresses were checked and verified to be correct at the time
of publication. Because of the dynamic nature of the Web, some addresses
and links may have changed since publication and may no longer be valid.

Table of Contents

FOREWORD BY
KYLE ZIMMER
PRESIDENT, FIRST BOOK

HUMANITY IS POWERED by stories. From our earliest days as thinking beings, we employed every available tool to tell each other stories. We danced, drew pictures on the walls of our caves, spoke, and sang. All of this extraordinary effort was designed to entertain, recount the news of the day, explain natural occurrences—and then gradually to build religious and cultural traditions and establish the common bonds and continuity that eventually formed civilizations. Stories are the most powerful force in the universe; they are the primary element that has distinguished our evolutionary path.

Our love of the story has not diminished with time. Enormous segments of societies are devoted to the art of storytelling. Book sales in the United States alone topped $26 billion last year; movie studios spend fortunes to create and promote stories; and the news industry is more pervasive in its presence than ever before.

There is no mystery to our fascination. Great stories are magic. They can introduce us to new cultures, or remind us of the nobility and failures of our own, inspire us to greatness or scare us to death; but above all, stories provide human insight on a level that is unavailable through any other source. In fact, stories connect each of us to the rest of humanity not just in our own time, but also throughout history.

This special magic of books is the greatest treasure that we can hand down from generation to generation. In fact, that spark in a child that comes from books became the motivation for the creation of my organization, First Book, a national literacy program with a simple mission: to provide new books to the most disadvantaged children. At present, First Book has been at work in hundreds of communities for over a decade. Every year children in need receive millions of books through our organization and millions more are provided through dedicated literacy institutions across the United States and around the world. In addition, groups of people dedicate themselves tirelessly to working with children to share reading and stories in every imaginable setting from schools to the streets. Of course, this Herculean effort serves many important goals. Literacy translates to productivity and employability in life and many other valid and even essential elements. But at the heart of this movement are people who love stories, love to read and want desperately to ensure that no one misses the wonderful possibilities that reading provides.

When thinking about the importance of books, there is an overwhelming urge to cite the literary devotion of great minds. Some have written of the magnitude of the importance of literature. Amy Lowell, an American poet, captured the concept when she said, "Books are more than books. They are the life, the very heart and core of ages past, the reason why men lived and worked and died, the essence and quintessence of their lives." Others have spoken of their personal obsession with books, as in Thomas Jefferson's simple statement: "I live for books." But more compelling, perhaps, is the almost instinctive excitement in children for books and stories.

Throughout my years at First Book, I have heard truly extraordinary stories about the power of books in the lives of children. In one case, a homeless child, who had been bounced from one location to another, later resurfaced—and the only possession that he had fought to keep was the book he was given as part of a First Book distribution months earlier. More recently, I met a child who, upon receiving the book he wanted, flashed a big smile and said, "This is my big chance!" These snapshots reveal the true power of books and stories to give hope and change lives.

As these children grow up and continue to develop their love of reading, they will owe a profound debt to those volunteers who reached out to them—a debt that they may repay by reaching out to spark the next generation of readers. But there is a greater debt owed by all of us—a debt to the storytellers, the authors, who have bound us together, inspired our leaders, fueled our civilizations, and helped us put our children to sleep with their heads full of images and ideas.

WHO WROTE THAT? is a series of books dedicated to introducing us to a few of these incredible individuals. While we have almost always honored stories, we have not uniformly honored storytellers. In fact, some of the most important authors have toiled in complete obscurity throughout their lives or have been openly persecuted for the uncomfortable truths that they have laid before us. When confronted with the magnitude of their written work or perhaps the daily grind of our own, we can forget that writers are people. They struggle through the same daily indignities and dental appointments, and they experience the intense joy and bottomless despair that many of us do. Yet somehow they rise above it all to deliver a powerful thread that connects us all. It is a rare honor to have the opportunity that these books provide to share the lives of these extraordinary people. Enjoy.

The Dutch Twins

Lucy Fitch Perkins

Cover of The Dutch Twins *(1911), by Lucy Fitch Perkins, the book Beverly Cleary says changed her outlook on books and reading. She read the entire book in one day, a day she called one of the most exciting of her life. She became an eager reader after reading this book, which followed the adventures of Kit and Kat Vedder.*

1

Blackbird to Bluebird

BEVERLY CLEARY NEARLY didn't learn how to read. The much-loved, world-famous children's author was once a frustrated six-year-old struggling to read stories that were too boring to bother reading under the guidance of a strict teacher. Her unhappiness was surprising. Just a few years before, Beverly's mother had founded the first library in the family's small Oregon hometown, Yamhill, and Beverly was entranced by the fairy tales and stories her mother read to her at bedtime. Then the family moved to Portland, and Beverly was able to visit a large city library for the first time. "Mother chose books to read aloud to me, and I ran my fingers along the spines of thousands of books I would soon be able to read aloud myself."[1] These were the exciting stories Beverly imagined learning to read when she began first grade.

Yet her reading book, called a primer, was no fun at all. "We had no bright beckoning book covers with words such as 'fun,' 'adventure,' or 'horizon' to tempt us on. . . . Our primer looked grim. Its olive-green cover with its black lettering bore the symbol of a beacon of light, presumably to guide us and to warn us of the dangers that lay within."[2] The stories inside were about children unlike "any children [I] knew, and even the animals were unrealistically depicted."[3] Beverly did not expect, and was very disappointed, to find herself reading simple sentences such as, "See kitty" and "I have a ball."[4]

School became a place of dread mixed with boredom. Beverly's teacher, Miss Falb, enforced bewildering rules. She ordered Beverly to write with her right hand instead of her left, and both hands burned from the attention of Miss Falb's metal-tipped bamboo pointer. Yet Beverly felt unable to confide in her parents. Her mother, the descendent of pioneers who had braved starvation and disease to settle in Oregon, would sternly remind her, "Show some spunk and remember your pioneer ancestors!"[5]

When Beverly fell ill with chicken pox and then smallpox, it was a relief to avoid reading lessons at school. But her long absence caused her to fall even further behind. To Beverly's dismay, her class had been divided into three groups of readers: Bluebirds, the best readers, were allowed to sit by the window; Redbirds sat in the middle of the classroom; and Blackbirds, the poorest readers, were forced to sit by the blackboard. "I was not surprised to be a Blackbird," Beverly later wrote.[6] Blackbirds were forced to recite simple words "from the despised and meaning-less word lists" every day in front of the entire class.[7] Her struggle to read seemed to cast a shadow over everything else in her life. "From a country child who had never known fear, I became a city child consumed by fear."[8] Beverly felt intense relief when she was able to recognize a word. At the end of the school year Beverly had barely passed the first grade.

"THE MOST EXCITING DAY OF MY LIFE"

Second grade was an improvement over first grade. Beverly learned how to read, but she did not learn to love books. Aware of her pupil's difficulties, her "calm, gentle, kind" teacher gave her undivided attention to Beverly.[9] They practiced reading actual stories, not a babyish list of words. Beverly was soon able to read on her own, but she still refused to open a book outside of class. Her mother, a passionate reader, puzzled over her daughter's lack of interest. Beverly was stubborn; not once during second grade did she read outside of school. There was just one exception, the silent movies at the local Roseway Theater. "All I wanted to read were the titles of the silent movies . . . I learned to read fast, before the titles disappeared from the screen."[10]

Third grade began without Beverly changing her mind about reading. Her mother, however, persisted in trying to reawaken Beverly's love for books, giving Beverly children's books checked out from the family's church. One dreary, rainy Sunday, when "the outside world drizzled [and] the inside world was heavy with the smell of pot roast and my father's Sunday after-dinner cigar," Beverly found herself so bored that she picked up one of the books checked out by her mother, *The Dutch Twins* by Lucy Fitch

Perkins.[11] The story, about two regular children and their funny adventures, was a revelation. "Here was a book with a story in which something happened. . . . With rising elation, I read on."[12] As an only child, Beverly found "the idea of twins fascinating. A twin would never be lonely. Here was a whole book about twins, a boy and a girl who lived in Holland but who had experiences a girl in Portland, Oregon, could share."[13] She found herself engrossed in the story and "happy in a way I had not been since starting school."[14] Beverly was allowed to stay awake past bedtime to finish the book, a happy conclusion to a day she later called one of the most exciting of her life.

REMEMBERING THE BLACKBIRDS

Soon Beverly was devouring all the children's books at her local library. She enjoyed fairy tales, but "what she really wanted to read were stories where children could solve problems by themselves."[15] That year the local newspaper promised a free book to any child who would write a review. Beverly's mother volunteered her, the review was published, along with a photo of Beverly, and "suddenly I was a school celebrity."[16] The Blackbird was now a published writer.

Beverly went on to write many books, including *Henry Huggins*, *Socks*, and *Dear Mr. Henshaw*; two autobiographies; historical fiction; young-love novels; plays; television scripts; and picture books for toddlers. Her best-known character, Ramona Quimby, is the star of the *Ramona* books, which have spanned four decades. Beverly is the recipient of nearly every award a children's author can receive and many other honors. Her books have been translated into many languages, and television shows based on Henry Huggins have aired in Japan, Denmark, and Sweden. PBS broadcast a ten-part series based on Ramona, and all three books about Beverly's motorcycle-riding mouse, Ralph S. Mouse, have been adapted for television movies.

Yet the successful author never forgot what it felt like to be a Blackbird. Although Beverly's characters are fictional, they are rooted in her childhood experiences. She has never shied away from remembering the difficult or confusing parts of childhood, as well as the fun. Her books, Beverly has written, are about "the little everyday experiences that do not seem important to adults, but which are so terribly important to children."[17] The experiences include hoping for a genuinely scary costume for Halloween, fearing the sinister shadows in a dark bedroom, wishing for clothing and shoes that aren't hand-me-downs, and sadness over a favorite teacher's disapproval.

CHRONICLING EVERYDAY LIFE

As an author, Beverly contrasts the ordinary—the long, dull hours of a rainy Saturday—with the subtle revelations of growing up. Headstrong Ramona Quimby often finds herself "angry and frustrated, but she struggles to learn the self-control and patience her parents and teachers expect."[18] Leigh Botts, the protagonist in *Dear Mr. Henshaw*, dwells on larger concerns, like whether he is the reason his parents divorced, as well as day-to-day worries, such as the culprit who steals treats from his lunch. Beverly's point-of-view shows how Ramona and Leigh see their situations, not as an adult would. They grow and learn naturally, not from lessons an adult provides.

No doubt Beverly's books remain so popular simply because they are fun to read. She shows her readers that "growing up is never easy, but it can be funny."[19] In

Ramona the Pest, when Ramona learns to sing the "The Star-Spangled Banner," she pronounces "the dawn's early light" as the "dawnzer lee light." She is confused, but decides that "dawnzer" is another word for lamp. She attempts to impress her family by asking to turn on the dawnzer, to the great amusement of her sister and parents. In this instance, Beverly's shows both the adult perspective

Did you know...

1916, the year Beverly (Bunn) Cleary is born, Woodrow Wilson is reelected president of the United States. Much of Europe is embroiled in the First World War and over one million soldiers die in the Battle of the Somme. Irish nationalists lead the 1916 Easter Uprising, a rebellion against British rule. The first child labor law is passed in the United States. The first woman is appointed to the U.S. House of Representatives and Louis Brandeis is the first Jewish justice appointed to the U.S. Supreme Court. The United States launches its first-ever air combat mission against Mexican revolutionary Pancho Villa. The Boston Red Sox win the World Series. Notable births that year include actors Gregory Peck, Kirk Douglas, and Jackie Gleason; Francis Crick, co-discoverer of the DNA structure; and *Willy Wonka and the Chocolate Factory* author Roald Dahl. Other events in 1916 include the invention of fortune cookies and Orange Crush soda.

—the humor of the mispronunciation—and Ramona's perspective, who is angry and perplexed about being laughed at.

From her first book, Beverly eschewed fantastic situations for believable, but highly comic stories. In *Henry Huggins*, Henry is cast as a little boy in his school's Christmas pageant. Mortified when his nickname at school becomes "little boy," Henry tries desperately to get out of the role, with no luck. On the eve of the pageant, Henry's dog, Ribsy, accidentally knocks over a can of green paint, which lands squarely on Henry. His face and hair stained green, Henry avoids playing the little boy and is cast as the Green Elf instead.

FUNNY STORIES

Beverly Cleary has noted that children like jokes and funny stories because they help "him or her realize that reading is a worthwhile experience. . . . The first books to catch the imagination of children who have escaped the reading circle and are ready to discover the pleasures of reading have been simply written humorous books."[20] Older readers are able to look back and relate to the funny stories that may remind them of their own childhood.

Before she ever published a book, Beverly believed the world lacked proper stories about ordinary children growing up and having fun. She once wrote, "[A]dults feel the purpose of any book is to teach. . . . Children would learn so much more if they were allowed to relax, enjoy a story, and discover what it is they want or need from books."[21] She learned this lesson as a librarian fresh from college in a small Washington town. A nun had come in for help, unable to interest her group of boys in reading. One of the students asked Beverly, "Where are the books about children like us?"[22] She never forgot that question. Beverly herself had wished for "funny stories about the sort of children who lived in my neighborhood."[23] When she finally sat down to write what became *Henry Huggins*, Beverly remembered her mother's advice that people like simple, funny stories, and as well as the question that she had been asked so long ago.

Growing up, Beverly resented stories that tried to teach her a lesson. She has said that such books don't respect that children can think for themselves. Her list of what *not* to write about includes:

> any book in which a child accepted the wisdom of an adult and reformed, any book in which a child reformed at all, any book in which problems were solved by a long-lost rich relative turning up in the last chapter, any book in which a family was grateful for the gift of a basket of groceries, usually on Christmas Eve, or any book in which a child turned out to be a lord of the manor or heir to a fortune. These things did not happen in my neighborhood."[24]

In *Ramona the Pest*, five-year-old Ramona means to please her parents and teacher, but so often she ends up doing exactly what *she* pleases. She simply can't understand why she should resist pulling a classmate's beautiful blond curls. At the end of the book, Ramona is essentially the same. Over the next six books she becomes aware that adults sometimes see her as a show-off and a pest, and as part of growing up she learns to think of others, not just herself. Yet throughout the books the point of view is always Ramona's. The reader can understand Ramona's thoughts and feelings, which Beverly never trivializes. Part of the richness of Beverly's books is that the characters are allowed to be both wise and foolish. Leigh Botts realizes that his father loves him but won't always be a responsible parent. Ralph S. Mouse chews his way through a basket of clean laundry but later carries aspirin in his mouth to a sick human friend. Socks the cat struggles with jealousy over his owner's new baby. By mining her own emotions and thoughts for stories, Beverly's books can truly be said to have universal appeal, a "chronicle of everyday life in the twentieth century."[25]

Yamhill, Oregon, in 1900. Beverly Cleary grew up on a farm outside of the town. Her uncle was the mayor, her father was on the town council, and her mother started Yamhill's first library. Cleary lived there until she was six and the family moved to Portland.

2

Farm Girl, City Life

BEVERLY CLEARY WAS born Beverly Bunn on April 12, 1916 in McMinnville, Oregon. A century earlier, her great-grandparents had left New York to head west in covered wagons. Beverly's great-grandfather Jacob Hawn built grain mills, so he set out with his family in 1843 in search of "outposts of civilization in need of mills for grain or lumber."[26] Hundreds of pioneer families traveled with them. The families hunted buffalo for meat and traded with Indians, who referred to the pioneers as "Bostons."[27] The journey was difficult, but when the Hawns finally settled, Jacob helped build the first mill in what would later become the state of Oregon.

Beverly's paternal grandparents, John and Marion Bunn, settled in Yamhill, Oregon, building one of the finest houses in the area and raising eight children, including Beverly's father, Chester. As the child of pioneers, he was raised to be independent. When he was fifteen, Chester was sent to the butcher shop to buy steak. Instead, he traveled to eastern Oregon and worked on ranches for a summer. When he returned three months later, all his father asked was, "Did you bring the beefsteak?"[28]

Beverly's mother, Mabel Atlee, a native of Michigan, lived a more sheltered existence. She became a schoolteacher and in 1905 was hired by mail to teach in Oregon. Her parents moved to Oregon a few years later, opening a general store. Visiting her parents one day, Mabel encountered a man sitting on the steps of the store, "a tall handsome young man wearing a white sweater and eating a pie, a whole pie."[29] Chester and Mabel married in December 1907. The young couple moved to Yamhill, where Chester took over the family farm and Mabel adjusted with some difficulty to life of a farmer's wife. Shortly before Beverly's birth, Mabel traveled by train to McMinnville, where the nearest hospital was located. The hospital was experiencing a nursing shortage, so Mabel kept busy before she gave birth by dusting and helping around the hospital.[30]

"REMEMBER YOUR PIONEER ANCESTORS"

In her memoir, *A Girl from Yamhill*, Beverly described her earliest memories: her father on a horse; the farm's orchard; the woodshed and icehouse; the cornfield and, past the house, a field of wheat; and the church bells and fire bell ringing loudly throughout Yamhill to commemorate the end of World War One. During one early Thanksgiving, the white tablecloth, loaded down with food, filled Beverly with longing. She found a bottle of blue ink, dipped her hands in it, and made handprints all over the cloth. "All I recall is my satisfaction in marking with ink on that white surface."[31]

Being the descendent of pioneers was trying at times. Whenever Beverly complained, her parents would admonish her to "remember your pioneer ancestors."[32] If Beverly fell down or hurt herself, he father would say, "Buck up, kid. You'll pull through. Your pioneer ancestors did." Not surprisingly, she "came to resent those exemplary people."[33] Her parents also admonished her to "never be afraid."[34] The only child of two hard-working farmers, Beverly was expected to take care of herself. No one minded her getting dirty or exploring all corners of the farm. On sunny afternoons Beverly would sit beneath the apple tree, taking a single bite out of each "cream-colored apple with pink cheeks," then throwing it away.[35] The first bite of the apple tasted best, a belief that Ramona Quimby later expressed. Beverly also tripped chickens and dropped worms into the mouths of baby birds. One cold morning she stood by the warm stove and dared to touch it, burning herself. Neither parent stopped her. "'She has to learn sometime' was all Father said. Neither parent offered any sympathy. I had to learn."[36]

Early on, Beverly proved she had plenty of imagination. Using an orange to demonstrate, her father taught her that the world was round and if someone walked in a straight line they could walk around the entire planet and arrive back at the same spot. That spring Beverly, fascinated by the idea of walking around the planet, set off. She got as far as the edge of the farm before she was spotted by her father, who explained how large the earth really was. After hearing her mother say that there was a pot of gold at the end of every rainbow, Beverly tried to find the end of a rainbow, with no luck.

A settler with his wagon train and family on his way to the western United States in the early nineteenth century. Beverly Cleary's ancestors were pioneers, as her parents often reminded her, and some of the first settlers to reach Oregon from the Oregon Trail. Her great-grandfather Jacob Hawn left New York in 1843 and helped build the first mill in what would later become the state of Oregon. Whenever things got tough, Cleary's parents told her to "Remember your pioneer ancestors."

Inside the Bunn farmhouse and under her mother's watchful gaze, Beverly felt she had far less freedom. There were many rules. She was expected to be quiet and polite when the family went into town. Although she wanted to look inside the saloon, it wasn't what "nice" young ladies did. Beverly wondered why her mother was concerned about being nice when she did so much dirty and back-breaking work on the farm that could never be considered nice. Even as a child, Beverly noticed the contradictions in the endless rules.

BEVERLY'S FIRST BOOKS

Mabel, who missed having female friends nearby, read voraciously and eventually instilled in her daughter the same love of books. Beverly's earliest encounter with a book was a memorable one:

> When I was four years old . . . a neighbor showed me a picture book which so delighted me that she invited me to look at it any time I pleased. Unfortunately, her bachelor son had a made a deal to sell me for a nickel to another neighbor, Quong Hop, who was planning to return to China to die. To reach the book I had to pass Quong Hop's house, and since I did not want to go to China, but I did want to see that book, I snaked on my stomach through tall grass and arrived damp with spitbug spit. Alert for the son's footsteps so I could hide in the pantry, I perched on a kitchen chair and studied the pictures. . . . "[37]

At home Mabel told Beverly every story she could remember, from "Little Red Riding Hood" and "Three Little Pigs" to all the poetry she could recite. She read Beverly catchphrases from magazine advertisements, and Beverly loved the Campbell Soup twins, "chubby and happy, always playing together."[38] Beverly owned only two books, *Mother Goose* and *The Story of the Three Bears*. "Mother read both books until I had them memorized," Beverly later wrote.[39]

Hungry for more books, Mabel decided to start Yamhill's first library. Money was short in the community, but she persisted. Finally a room, shelves, and books were donated, though to Beverly's dismay the library opened without any children's books. Crates of books finally arrived from the Oregon State Library, and children's books with them. Beverly snapped up *More English Fairy Tales*, which had to be pried out of her hands at bedtime, and Beatrix Potter's books. The library was very popular, even though Beverly remembered it as a "dingy room filled with shabby leather-covered chairs and smelling of stale cigar smoke."[40]

When she tired of reading to Beverly, her mother tried to teach her how to read. Beverly flat-out refused. "I wanted to learn to read in the real school with other children, not in our kitchen alone with Mother."[41]

YAMHILL TO PORTLAND

Beverly's family was an important part of Yamhill—her uncle was the mayor, her father was on the town council, and her mother was a librarian. Church picnics, town dances, and Fourth of July parades were highlights of her childhood. Yet troubles on the farm were more significant than Beverly knew. When she was six, her father's abundant harvest of "heavy wheat, laden fruit trees, woolly sheep, fat hogs, [and] cows that gave rich milk" failed to sell for enough money.[42] Not long after her father announced he was quitting the farm. Mabel, who never enjoyed being a farmer's wife, was relieved. The family placed their posses-sions on a truck and boarded a train for Portland, Oregon, heading toward a new life. Beverly wasn't sad to leave Yamhill as "home was wherever my parents lived."[43] She looked forward to Portland and the possibility of children to play with. Her earliest years, however, had provided a sense of certainty and order that proved difficult to recapture: "Even though adults had trouble, I was secure. Yamhill had taught me that the world was safe and a beautiful place, where children were treated with kindness, patience, and tolerance. Everyone loved little girls. I was sure of that."[44]

With little formal education, Beverly's father was only able to find a job as the night guard at a bank. The Bunns moved into a six-bedroom house that felt warm and cozy after the large, drafty farmhouse. Portland looked exotic to Beverly: concrete sidewalks, streetcars, elevators, roller skates, and a large children's room at the city library. For the first time, Beverly "had children to play with who could be summoned by standing in front of their houses and yelling their names."[45] There was an entirely new world of games and toys and discover. Beverly and her friends pounded rose petals with rocks and soaked them in water, attempting to make perfume. They smashed bricks into dust in a game known as Brick Factory. They made stilts with coffee cans and twine, shouting names at children on neighboring streets and bloodying their knees after the twine snapped.

Did you know...

Many of Beverly Cleary's books are set in Portland, Oregon, where Beverly grew up. Portland is home to Henry Huggins, Ramona and Beezus Quimby, Otis Spofford, and Ellen Tibbits. The city is the largest in Oregon and is bordered by rivers and a mountain. Once a forest used by the local Chinook Indians to fuel their campfires, the area was named "Stumptown" by the first settlers because "of all the tree stumps that littered the ground." Today Portland is a major exporter of wheat and lumber and has been dubbed "the City of Roses" for its beautiful rose gardens. [Kelly 52]

When Beverly's father brought home her first-grade primer, she inhaled "the new-book smell, eager to join other children in reading from them."[46] The first day of school was blurred with excitement, children, and new sensations. Excitement turned to confusion and then unhappiness as Beverly discovered she did not enjoy what she was supposed to be reading. Her teacher, Mrs. Falb, chastised Beverly for writing with her left hand, and later placed her in the Blackbirds group for the class's slowest readers. Noticing Beverly's anxiety, her mother paid the class a visit. She did not see the Mrs. Falb that Beverly knew; in front of her mother, the teacher was kind and gentle. Beverly protested to her mother that it was an act, but Mabel urged her daughter to remember her pioneer spunk. The incident with Mrs. Falb stung her. "I learned a bitter lesson of childhood —that an adult can be a hypocrite."[47]

MOLDING HER CHARACTER

As Beverly entered third grade, the family moved again to a smaller house near the Portland city limits. The house was just over one block north of Klickitat Street, the street that would later be immortalized as the home of Henry Huggins and Beezus and Ramona Quimby. The neighborhood was rural, with houses farther apart and fewer children to play with. It was in this quieter atmosphere that Beverly, on a rainy, boring Sunday, began reading again. Her only difficulty in school was now the dreaded multiplication tables. That year, Beverly was not selected to be one of the lilac blossoms in the third grade's spring dance recital because she was too short. To her dismay, her favorite teacher called Beverly a nuisance when she volunteered as a substitute. The word nuisance stung her terribly, and she later included the incident in *Ramona the Pest*. That summer the family moved again. Beverly passed the time making new friends and going to the movies with her parents. Her favorites were the "Our Gang" comedies. "To me these comedies were about neighborhood children playing together, something I wanted to read about in books. I longed for books about the children of Hancock Street."[48]

Beverly's mother had a different idea about what her daughter needed. That summer she decided it was time to "mold my character. I was too old to call her Mamma. I was to call her Mother. Her rules followed me around the house like mosquitoes. 'Use your head.' 'Stand on your own two feet.' 'Use your ingenuity.' 'Never borrow.' 'Use your imagination.' And, of course, 'Remember your pioneer ancestors,' who used their heads, stood on their own two feet, always stuck to it, never borrowed."[49] Her mother's favorite word with Beverly was "try." There was the occasional bright side to so much trying. A contest was announced with a prize of $2 for the best essay about an animal. On the final day of the contest, Beverly was declared the winner. She was then informed that no one else had entered. "This incident was one of the most valuable lessons in writing I ever learned. Try! Others will talk about writing but may never get around to trying."[50]

At night Beverly overheard her parents having serious, hushed conversations. Her father began to lose his temper over small things. To Beverly, these rages were a mystery. She later understood that he hated his job and, without much training or formal education, had little chance of finding another one. Tensions also mounted between Beverly and her mother. They fought over the high brown shoes and uncomfortable woolen underwear Beverly resisted wearing. Her mother's lack of affection and constant monitoring confused and pained Beverly. Now in the fifth grade, she

had made her first best friend, Mary Dell. Mary's house was
a wholly different atmosphere from Beverly's. Mary's mother
"seemed happy and carefree, often with a paintbrush in her
hand."[51] Mary's mother did something else quite different
from Beverly's mother: "She kissed her daughters. This
filled me with longing."[52] Beverly found the nerve to
inform her mother about the affection she had witnessed.
"Mother laughed, pulled me to her, and gave me a hug and
a kiss—a sweet, isolated moment. It was never repeated."[53]
Beverly often thought back to that moment, wondering
why her mother would not hug and kiss her. "My house
was always cold and drab compared to Mary Dell's house;
Mother was always tired and nervous."[54]

The summer before sixth grade money was very tight
and Beverly's mother began working from home, selling
magazine subscriptions. "When I came home from school
that dark and dreary winter, I felt as if Mother, bundled up
in an old sweater, had shut me out by endlessly repeating
the merits of McCall's to strangers over the phone."[55]
Beverly escaped through books, particularly the Greek myth
about Persephone, the daughter of a Greek goddess, who is
captured by the god of the underworld when she stops to
admire a beautiful field of flowers. Beverly saw her own
life as the dark underworld, although as she read the story
again and again, she "came to understand that we cannot
expect flowers to bloom continuously in life."[56]

FINDING HER FUTURE

The family's situation improved a little when Beverly's
father finally sold the family farm. With the money, the
family enjoyed some prosperity, bought their first car, had
Beverly's teeth straightened, and moved once again, back
near Klickitat Street. Now in seventh grade, Beverly's class

studied reading with an exciting young librarian named Miss Smith who encouraged students to use their imagination. Once she surprised her class by having them write an essay on the spot as though they lived in George Washington's time. To Beverly's surprise, the next day Miss Smith read her essay aloud to the class. The class was next assigned to write an essay about their favorite book character. Beverly had so many, she decided to write about a girl who travels to Bookland and interviews her favorite characters. "As the rain beat against the windows, a feeling of peace came over me as I wrote far beyond the required length of the essay,"[57] After the class turned in their essays, Beverly watched Miss Smith go through the papers. She selected one and began reading it aloud; it was Beverly's. At the end of the essay, Miss Smith announced to the class, "When Beverly grows up, she should write children's books."[58]

Beverly was shocked. She had not thought about what lay in the distant future, "a misty time I rarely even thought about."[59] "Now I was not only being praised in front of the whole class but was receiving approval that was to give direction to my life." Beverly took her teacher's wisdom very seriously and shared the revelation with her mother. Her mother pointed out that a writer must have another way to earn a living. Beverly's decision was easily made. "The Rose City Branch Library—quiet, tastefully furnished, filled with books and flowers—immediately came to mind. I wanted to work in such a place, so I would become a librarian."[60] Once she made up her mind, Beverly didn't waver.

THE GREAT DEPRESSION

Beverly began eighth grade in 1929 with a growing realization that the world was changing around her. She was preoccupied with boys, "horrible" boys, and the "fast" girls in her class who wore lipstick and refused to stay after school for class assignments, even though Beverly was too nervous about her grades to be anything but a "teacher-pleaser."[61] At home her parents talked in worried whispers about things Beverly did not care about, "high tariffs, the stock market, Wall Street banking."[62] Portland banks had begun to close, and that winter, Beverly's father didn't receive a much-needed bonus. While Beverly and her class-mates learned how to "write checks, borrow money, read interest tables, and compound interest semiannually," the biggest financial disaster in American history unfolded. In October 1929, the stock marked crashed and "except for school, everything seemed to come to a halt."[63] Yet life did continue. Beverly graduated eighth grade that summer and as each student crossed the stage to receive their diploma they also were handed their first adult library card, "a symbol marking the end of childhood."[64]

Beverly's father lost his job as bank guard and began a grim search for work, any kind of work at all. In her auto-biography Beverly recounted the sense of futility that fell over her household:

> Every workday morning he left the house. Late in the after-noon he came home with his shoulders sagging, his footsteps heavy.
>
> Mother searched his face. "Well?" she always questioned.
>
> "Nothing" was his answer. Everywhere men were being laid off, not hired.[65]

In the dark days of the Depression, money had to be stretched as far as possible, food had to be made to last. When Beverly's mother ran out of vanilla for baking desserts, she began using a large bottle of almond-flavored cornstarch. "We ate almond-flavored cake; almond-flavored cornstarch, tapioca, and bread pudding; almond-flavored cookies and custard. Mother even made almond-flavored fudge, until she used up all the chocolate. . . . The Depression, for me, took on the flavor of almond."[66] When their tea ran out, her parents drank hot water with dinner. Beverly's mother entered as many contests as possible, trying to win prize money. She won honorable mention and was awarded $2 for naming a new brand of bread. The family cancelled the weekly newspaper and Beverly's father learned how to sharpen his razor blade instead of buying a new one. He quit smoking to save on the cost of tobacco and finally sold the family's car.

Beverly continued to display her gift for writing in high school. For one class she wrote a story about a boy who was accidentally dyed green, saving him from performing in the school Christmas pageant. She received good grades, and her better papers were read aloud in class. After several months without a job, Beverly's father found work managing a safe-deposit vault. The paycheck was smaller than that of his last job, but the family could now afford food and mortgage payments. Once the strain over money and employment lifted, Beverly and her mother began fighting again. Following one battle, Beverly's father slapped Beverly across the mouth after she called her mother a name. Parents were to be obeyed, he told her firmly. Beverly felt guilt over her mixed feelings. She wanted so badly to make decisions without her mother attempting to control her every move. Yet her parents had sacrificed their own happiness to give her braces and send her to summer camp during the Depression. "Although Mother and I had an uncomfortable relationship, her softer moments revealed her hopes for me that told me she might love me even though she showed no tenderness toward me."[67]

THE LETTER

Their rift deepened the following year. Beverly began to notice boys, although she wasn't quite certain what to do with them. Over Christmas break, Beverly and her best friend Claudine snuck into a college-age dance where, to Beverly's surprise, a young man asked her to dance. Eager to see her daughter feted by young men, Beverly's mother enrolled her in dance classes and began taking her to Friday night dances. At one of those dances she met a young man, identified in her autobiography with a fictitious name, Gerhart. While her mother delighted over the older, gainfully employed Gerhart, Beverly felt uncomfortable around him; he was controlling, they had nothing in common, and he treated her hobbies with disdain. Beverly's lack of interest didn't stop Gerhart from pursuing her, and he was encouraged by her mother to stop by their house often. One day at a stoplight, he gave Beverly her first kiss. "I had expected a kiss to feel more like the time in Yamhill when I stuck my finger in the electric socket, only nice. . . . I went along with Gerhart's occasional kisses, hoping they would get better."[68] Beverly was cast as the lead in a school play her junior year, and a kiss came at the end of the script. "I fell into the arms of Bob, who kissed me rather hastily as the curtain was lowered—but that kiss was long enough to let me know that there were better kissers in the world than Gerhart."[69]

Her senior year of high school, neighbors reminded Beverly and Claudine that these were supposed to be the happiest days of their life. They also hinted that there might be a June wedding for Beverly. In fact, Gerhart had proposed to Beverly and she turned him down. It was important to Beverly's mother, however, that life appear serene to outsiders. To Beverly's horror, she kept a diary of her daughter's life, recording every event as if it were positive. Gerhart was frequently invited over, even after Beverly broke off the relationship. Beverly was about to graduate, but it was clear that the family could not afford college. Beverly could not think of what she would do. Beverly's grades dropped during her senior year, since she was worn out and depressed from fights with her mother over Gerhart. One day, a letter arrived from Beverly's cousin Verna in California. The letter was an invitation for Beverly to come live with Verna's family the next year and attend junior college, which was tuition-free in California. Immediately, her mother dismissed the idea and Beverly herself did not take it seriously. It seemed impossible to hope that a solution to her problems could be so easily extended. Beverly watched as her classmates prepared for college, left out of the excitement they were swept up in. The "misty future" seemed more obscure than ever.

Then one night she overheard her parents talking urgently in the living room. She heard her mother protest whatever her father was saying, but did not hear his response. Beverly was called into the living room. Her father had decided that Beverly would live with Verna in southern California, and attend junior college. For the first time all year, "I had hope."[70] Many years later she reflected on her father's decision:

> Dad quietly observed Mother's relentless control over me, and my growing desperation. When escape was unexpectedly offered, he saw it as an opportunity, not only for a year of college, but as a way of ending my relationship with Gerhart. As I look back, I can see that my father . . . always understood what I wanted—roller skates, a hard sponge-rubber ball, a hemp jump rope, a bicycle, and now, freedom. I was leaving.[71]

The steps pictured here lead up to the University of California at Berkeley's main library. Beverly Cleary looks back fondly over the two years spent at Cal as "two of the most interesting years of my life," as well as being the place where she met her future husband, Clarence Cleary.

3

California

MIXED FEELINGS COURSED through Beverly during the long bus ride to California. Sadness toward her father, who had sold the family farm and taken jobs that did not challenge him, and guilt toward her mother, who seemed to want to live her life through Beverly. "Now I was the focus of my parents' hopes; I must be educated no matter what sacrifices had to be made. I longed to have my parents happy, to share, not sacrifice. The burden of guilt was heavy."[72]

Her first glimpses of California were disheartening: stifling heat and dry riverbeds. The view from the bus window soon revealed towns with exotic Spanish names, "lusty red" flowers growing in the dirt, a glimpse of the notorious prison Alcatraz.[73] Her destination, Ontario, proved to be the California of Beverly's imagination: willowy palms; orange, lemon, and avocado trees; clear blue skies. There were things she'd never seen before, like trash incinerators and patios.[74] Beverly settled in immediately with Verna's family—her husband Fred, their two children, Atlee and Virginia, and Fred's mother. "The whole family was pleasant, relaxed; no one was nervous, tense, or worried. No one mentioned anyone who had lost his job, the high cost of fuel, shoes that needed resoling, or any other Depression subject."[75] That first night the family took Beverly swimming, a novelty for her.

IDYLLIC DAYS

The students at the Chaffey Junior College were another welcome shock. They were less preoccupied with cliques and popularity than the students at Beverly's high school were and more concerned with comfort and perfecting their deep tans. It struck her as "a small, friendly high school with older students."[76] To her great surprise, a boy introduced himself to her the first day. Nothing so casual had ever happened to Beverly in high school, where the boys were either shy or show-offs. Beverly was shocked and delighted, and she and the boy, Paul, became good friends.

Classes were challenging, and one of Beverly's favorites was geology. "[The] class taught me that nothing on earth is stable. Mountains rise only to be worn down. Rivers change courses. Lakes appear; lakes evaporate. Fertile lands become desert. I left the geology classroom realizing that not only was the earth unstable, life, too, was constantly changing."[77] In her books, Beverly's characters are often eager to grow up. They complain that their lives are slow and boring, like trying to watch a mountain wear down. And yet their lives are constantly shifting, changing slowly, but always changing and moving closer to growing up.

Beverly discovered in a letter from her mother that Gerhart had driven 900 miles to see her but upon reaching Verna's house, realized Beverly would not want to see him. The worry and guilt that had followed Beverly down from Portland began to lift. She was enjoying herself, and the Depression itself seemed to recede in California. Food was less expensive, and no one worried about heating bills that were always a concern in rainy Portland. Beverly had rarely seen her father attempt housework, and she was impressed with the vigor that Fred applied to doing laundry. "Laughter at the dinner table was a new experience for me."[78] Verna and Fred didn't seem to mind their children trying out their independence.

For quite some time, life in California was idyllic and dream-like. Beverly and Paul went to school dances and afterwards talked long into the night about their lives and aspirations. She didn't wish for anything more than friendship from Paul, and she marveled that she could relate to a boy as easily as her female friends. One night while doing homework, the house shook from an earthquake, Beverly's first. In the spring the orange trees bloomed with life, "blossoms with perfume so sweet and so heavy that walking to school seemed dreamy and unreal." When the oranges decayed, the town "was as fragrant as a vast kettle of marmalade."[79]

"WHAT AM I GOING TO DO NOW?"

When her year in California was nearly over, Beverly asked Verna about staying longer. To her great disappointment, she was turned down. Verna's mother was coming to live with the family, and there wasn't room for two grandmothers and Beverly. She plaintively asked her diary, "What am I going to do now?" [80] Her last few weeks in California were as enjoyable as always, but after Verna and Fred drove her to the Greyhound bus station, Beverly burst into tears. "I had been so happy and now I faced a blank future. What would happen now?" [81]

Although the past year had changed her life, she hid this fact from her parents, who were so happy to see her return safely. That long summer at home, Beverly vacationed with her parents, but relaxing was impossible. There was no obvious solution to her problems, no certainty that she would ever be able to return to college. In desperation, Beverly dimly recalled a fellow Chaffey student from Washington named Norma, who had stayed with a faculty family and who had also not been invited back. What if she could find this girl and offer to share an apartment? While she contemplated how to track down Norma, the family learned that Verna's mother had died. Now that there was a room once again at Verna's house, Beverly and her parents hoped they would invite her back.

Did you know...

Beverly Cleary's other favorite setting for her books is California, where she has lived for many years. She attended the University of California and was living in Berkeley, California, when she wrote *Henry Huggins*. Berkeley later became home to the twins in *Mitch and Amy* and the setting for *Sister of the Bride*. Today Beverly and her husband live in Carmel, California, part of the Monterey Peninsula. Carmel is close to Pacific Grove, the setting for *Dear Mr. Henshaw* and *Strider*. The area is known for its beautiful, rugged scenery, and Pacific Grove is famous for its butterfly trees, which feature prominently in the books.

For whatever reason, they did not. Beverly knew vaguely where Norma lived and wrote her a letter. Norma responded immediately and enthusiastically. Norma's parents were fine with the two girls living together, and Beverly's parents also agreed. Verna found the girls a two-bedroom apartment with a monthly rent of $15. Now truly on her own, Beverly basked in her independence. She marveled at going to the market on her own and taking turns cooking with Norma. She went to the movies, football games, and dances, earning extra money by knitting lace patterns and correcting high school Latin papers. In Beverly's English class, the teacher had students write a 300-word story every day until someone earned an A. After a few weeks, Beverly finally earned an A for a story about an old man trying to sell violets in a Portland restaurant. Her hard work was rewarded when she was offered a substitute librarian job in the school library. She was elated.

CAL

As graduation loomed, Beverly's future was once again uncertain. Although she doubted that she could afford any further education, Beverly applied to the University of California at Berkeley (Cal) to complete her undergraduate degree in English. Cal had a graduate program for librarians, which Beverly hoped to be accepted into. The yearly tuition, however, was a steep $150. But when she was accepted, her parents told her they would manage somehow. "I learned later that my father, like many Depression fathers, borrowed on his life insurance."[82] Where Beverly might live was another gray area. Cal had an all-female dorm, Stebbins Hall, that provided free rooms and meals in exchange for a daily half-hour of work, but it was rumored to have a long waiting list.

Beverly was required to write a short story for her English final. "My trouble was I couldn't think of a plot. . . . Finally

I sat down in the rocking chair, placed my feet on the gas heater, and commanded myself: Write!"[83] The first thing that came to mind was her unhappy experience of learning to read, the shame and despair she felt. She received an A and read the story to her class. "Without knowing it, I had begun to write the story of my life."[84]

When Norma's parents drove the roommates back to the Pacific Northwest, they stopped at Cal so Beverly could visit Stebbins Hall. She talked to the house mother, who explained there was no possibility of being accepted for the fall, but "my look of despair and disappointment must have touched her because she kindly said that she would add my name to the waiting list."[85] Trying to think of something she could say so that the house mother would remember her, Beverly added that "if I should be accepted, I hoped I would be assigned a roommate who was a good student and who did not smoke. In the 1930s many girls took up smoking as soon as they went away to college."[86]

In late July a letter arrived at her parent's house. She had been accepted at Stebbins Hall for the fall semester. When she arrived by train on a foggy morning to San Francisco, "I felt academically confident. . . . In many other ways, however, I felt insecure. Did I have enough money, were my clothes right, would I make friends, would I choose the right courses?"[87]

It proved to be "two of the most interesting years of my life."[88] The girls in Stebbins Hall were the usual assortment of young women attending college for the first time: "Tall, short, shy, 'fast,' brilliant, struggling, colorless, beautiful, neat, sloppy, confident, brokenhearted. . . . Some, and I was one, were sure where they wanted to go but did not know if they could find the money to get there."[89] Her new roommate, Miriam, was putting herself through college with a scholarship awarded each year to the student from Utah with the highest grade point average; she had won twice. Their rooms were inspected once a week, and Beverly and her roommate were expected to dust furniture, clean the bathroom, and vacuum the rugs. When Stebbins Hall's monthly expenses were raised $6 per month for every girl, Beverly opened a skirt-shortening business for girls who couldn't afford the shorter dresses that were in fashion. Her imagination allowed her to remain independent, even when money was tight.

Beverly's housemates warned her about the final for English majors, known as the Comprehensive. Their worried tones left Beverly wondering what could be so difficult about an English test. The back of her course catalog explained: "The Comprehensive Final Examination must be taken at the end of the senior year. It will consist of two three-hour papers, the second of which will take the form of an essay. The examination will cover English literature from 1350 to 1900."[90]

CLARENCE

Social life at Cal centered around dances at local clubs, houses, or sororities and fraternities. When Beverly was a student, there were two and a half men to every woman. It was never difficult to attract dance partners. Beverly dated a bit, but never for long. Some of her dates were with men who didn't bother to mention that they weren't actually single. At one dance, "a tall, thin young man with black hair and blue eyes" asked her to dance.[91] His name was Clarence Cleary. Clarence was six years older than Beverly, studying economics and history, and was "kind, gentle, quiet, and, best of all, single. I made sure of that."[92] The Depression had lengthened Clarence's pursuit of education. He had hitchhiked to his first college and later worked in a dairy. When he lost that job because of the Depression, he went back to school. Men and women were strictly forbidden in each other's rooms, but Clarence and Beverly made a habit of walking together in the evening and Sunday afternoons. Gradually she stopped seeing other men. She began mentioning Clarence in letters to her parents. Once her mother found out Clarence's family was Catholic, however, she urged Beverly to stop seeing him. No one in their family had ever married a Catholic.

"UNIVERSAL HUMAN EXPERIENCE"

That year, Beverly took a course on the novel that influenced her more than any class ever had. It was here that she learned about writing a story. Not how to write, which Beverly intuitively understood, but what to write about. She'd never thought about what she might want to write about. One comment from her professor stuck: "The proper subject of the novel is universal human experience." To convey human experience in a realistic and appealing way, the author had to focus on "the minutiae of life."[93] Although she did not write on her own outside of school, her professor's ideas impressed her a great deal.

After an unpleasant encounter with a secretary at the library school, Beverly decided not to attend Cal's graduate program in library studies. The woman strongly implied that Beverly was not a good enough student to be accepted into the program, and the school had nothing to offer a children's librarian. Instead she applied to the University of Washington's graduate school of librarianship.

During the first semester of her second year, Beverly's grades sank from the As and Bs she normally earned to Bs and Cs. Her eyesight was failing and her mother, ashamed that her daughter needed glasses, insisted Beverly would have to drop out of school if she genuinely needed them. So Beverly studied on without glasses. Toward the end of the school year, the pressure Beverly and her classmates felt was nearly overwhelming. Clarence was about to graduate, and after so many years of school on so little money, he was no longer certain what he wanted to do with his life. On top of that, Beverly felt hopeless about getting into the University of Washington's graduate library school. She feared having to return home for good. One evening, Clarence suggested to Beverly that once he got a job, she could come be with him. They would get married. "I had not allowed myself to think of love and had always thought of marriage as something far in the future. Now, suddenly, I knew I loved and wanted to marry him."[94] She wrote to her parents that she would marry Clarence after receiving an advanced degree and working for a year. Her mother, aghast at the idea of Beverly marrying a Catholic, said she would not give the couple her approval. In the midst of so much turmoil, Beverly was accepted at the University of Washington.

THE COMPREHENSIVE

Her final semester Beverly studied as much as possible for the Comprehensive exam. The morning of the first part of the dreaded test, Beverly and her fellow English majors were "hollow-eyed, silent, and unsmiling."[95] Beverly found herself unable to concentrate. She thought of the letters from her mother, Clarence, anything but the test question. When she called the school secretary for the results, she was horrified to find out her grade was an E minus. "'What?' I asked, aghast. I had never heard of such a grade. 'A, B, C, D, E-,' she said. For a moment I thought she might go on down the alphabet to an even stranger grade, possibly K-."[96] Beverly faced the thought of spending the summer at Cal, studying to retake the test. With a sense of impending doom, she took the second part of the test, which consisted of one question: "Discuss the novel." This time Beverly fared better. She earned a B and her final grade on the Comprehensive exam averaged out to a D. She would graduate.

Sather Gate, a prominent landmark at University of California at Berkeley, in 1957. Beverly Cleary worked at the nearby Sather Gate Book Shop during the Christmas shopping season for several years in the 1940s. She became good friends with Quail Hawkins, an authority on children's literature who was in charge of the children's department of the Sather Gate Book Shop from 1926 until 1972.

4

Blossoming

THE SUMMER BEVERLY graduated from Cal, she worked as a chambermaid in Stebbins Hall and saw Clarence, who had taken a job in Sacramento, on weekends. She made beds and cleaned the bathrooms during the day and set the table for dinner and cut Jell-O into cubes for dessert at night. It wasn't glamorous work, but "I was happy to be self-supporting, standing on my own two feet for the summer."[97] One of the women staying at the dorm gave her the name of a local boardinghouse in Seattle. Soon Beverly had arranged to rent a room in Seattle for $8 a month.

Her grades at the University of Washington rose again to As and Bs, although she did receive a C in one class because she looked "bored."[98] Beverly reflected later that in the 1930s, students did not rebel against their professors, usually swallowing small injustices with a tight smile. However, she decided that "being a librarian was more interesting than learning to be one."[99] When not in class, Beverly studied on campus, stopped at a cheap diner or coffee shop for dinner, and then returned to the boarding house to study and write letters to her friends and family. "Letters prevented loneliness."[100] Most of her friends were either going to school, working, or recently married. Beverly's eyesight had deteriorated to the point where she experienced headaches while reading. This time, her mother gave in. At last wearing glasses, she "walked into a new world. I could see individual bricks on buildings, street signs were suddenly legible, lines on the sidewalks were sharper."[101]

Clarence traveled to Portland that winter to meet Beverly's mother. The experience was not pleasant. Her mother wore the same dress Beverly had worn the night she met Clarence and would not explain to her daughter why. Her mother was courteous, but the strain was obvious to all. Beverly's mood brightened during New Year's Eve dinner, when Clarence slipped a cigar band on her finger and told her one day he'd replace it with a ring.

LIBRARIAN-IN-TRAINING

That spring Beverly worked as a student librarian in Portland for a month. Because the weather was beautiful, no children came into the library. The experience was a disappointment with one exception. Traveling with a bookmobile up the Columbia River, Beverly at last encountered children and adults interested in books and reading. "Farmers' wives who waited with armloads of books greeted us like old friends. . . . We stopped at a sawmill town near Bridal Veil Falls where workers, wives, and children, all eager and friendly, came aboard. Returning to Portland, they stopped at the governor's mansion, where "smiling servants came out to exchange their books. It was a beautiful, encouraging day that restored my faith in librarianship."[102]

Upon her return, Beverly was devastated to learn that she'd received a bad report from the Portland library and would not be accepted to work there after graduation. The complaints were minor—she filed too slowly and appeared to be in poor health because she leaned too much—but they prevented her from working in the library system she had loved growing up. She felt "exhausted, a complete failure."[103] More bad news followed. Her favorite professor helped arrange for Beverly to take the entrance examination for the Los Angeles library system. She wrote to her parents asking for a loan, but her mother refused. Beverly suspected it was to keep her from Clarence. Asking Clarence for the money was out of the question as "in the world in which I had grown up, this would have been a shocking thing to do."[104] With Los Angeles out of the picture, Beverly wondered what she would do after graduation. She arrived home in Portland without one cent. "I was free of school, ready to go on with my life. All I needed was a job."[105]

The summer dragged on without any of Beverly's job applications being answered. When her high school friend Claudine suggested they stay at her parent's summer cabin, Beverly was happy to accept. "As I listened to the clang of horse-shoes, the shouts and splashes from the river, and smelled the wood smoke and coffee of campers and picnickers, the stress of five Depression years of college drained away, and I began to feel like myself again."[106] Beverly's parents arrived at the cabin one hot August night with a letter from a library in Yakima, Washington, with a vacancy. She traveled to Yakima for the interview, "a town of about ten thousand people with fruit orchards to the west, dry rolling country to the east, and dominated by a monument to the Depression, the rusting skeleton of an unfinished fourteen-story hotel. The thermometer in a filling station . . . registered 110 degrees."[107]

"WHERE ARE THE BOOKS ABOUT KIDS LIKE US?"

Two days later she was hired to work in the children's room and the adult department for $110 a month, a fortune to Beverly. She found a room at a local boardinghouse where all the other renters were men. They treated Beverly with affection, calling her the Widow after she wore a black dress, bringing her flowers, and taking her to a local swimming hole. The library staff members were equally warm and welcoming, as were the library patrons. Beverly adored the children of Yakima. "In a one-library town, the children's librarian meets all sorts of children: bright, healthy children of doctors and lawyers, children of unemployed millworkers, sad waifs whose poverty-stricken parents were past caring, garden-variety middle-class children such as those I had grown up with."[108] One group of "grubby" little boys came with their teacher, who could not interest them in reading. Beverly discovered there really weren't any books for young boys. "'Where are the books about kids like us?' they wanted to know."[109] It proved to be an important moment for Beverly. "I recalled my own childhood reading, when I longed for funny stories about the sort of children who lived in my neighborhood. What was the matter with authors? I had often wondered and now wondered again."[110]

With a steady paycheck Beverly was able to buy a portable typewriter, to be used to write her children's books. A book salesmen who had come to the library even told her she looked like someone who could write a book. "The trouble was, I didn't have time to write them. . . . I had too many other things to think about—letters to Clarence, stories to learn for story hour, books and library periodicals to read. Most of my evenings I read, read, read. There was so much I needed to learn, so many books to become acquainted with." [111]

Rather than write stories, she told tales to children during the library's story hours. Her first day, Beverly was struck with stage fright. But when one of her friends from the boarding house presented her with a flower to celebrate the occasion, she overcame her nerves. Over time she learned to shut out the other noise from the library—crying babies and adults who stopped to listen—and to concentrate on the faces of the children. Her confidence soaring, she read stories in the park during the summer and visited local schools to share stories.

MRS. CLEARY AND THE ARMY

At Christmas, Clarence came to Yakima and asked Beverly to marry him. "We kissed and without speaking rose and began to dance to the music on the radio." [112] They decided to marry the following December. Knowing her parents would not approve, she waited several months to tell them. When she did, they were angry and refused to announce her engagement. Beverly pressed on, telling the head librarian she would leave Yakima that winter. The summer of 1940, Beverly and Clarence decided not to wait any longer and were married in Las Vegas. She was now Beverly Cleary. In December she said goodbye to her friends at the library and boarding house and moved to Sacramento.

Before long, Clarence took another job and the couple moved to Oakland. Without a job, Beverly visited the Sather Gate Book Shop in Berkley to read the latest children's books.

She struck up a conversation with one of the booksellers, who jumped to hire Beverly for the Christmas rush. She was soon commuting by two buses and a streetcar every day but Sunday for $18 a week. She did this for every Christmas for the next four years. During her first year at Sather Gate Book Shop, Pearl Harbor was bombed and America entered World War II. Beverly and Clarence decided she needed a full-time job so she could support herself if Clarence was drafted.

Beverly found a job as a librarian at the army base in Oakland. "I had a feeling that life in the Yakima boarding house full of men had been basic training for my new army life."[113] It wasn't Beverly's idea of a typical library. Soldiers played ping-pong nearby and jukeboxes shared the cement floors with bookshelves and uncomfortable tables and benches. Some of the men who worked night duty slept on the library's couches. She talked to soldiers from all over the country; she met a bootlegger, professional gamblers, a convict, and lawyers. At that time, the army was segregated by race, but Beverly and her fellow librarian opened their library to all men. Although she liked listening to the men, the difficult commute to work and the long hours at the base surrounded by exhausted, disheartened men took their toll. When Beverly was offered a librarian position at a nearby hotel that had been converted into a wartime hospital, she took it. During her interview, the commanding officer who oversaw the hospital patted her on the bottom. He then informed her that the soldiers could only come to the door of the library to return books and ask for more. None would be allowed in the library. "I was speechless. Then I thought of the rallying cry of the Office of Librarianship of the 9th Service Command: 'Make adversity work for you.' A rich opportunity of adversity lay ahead, if I could make it work."[114] The library was dimly lit, with bookcases built so high the top shelves could not be reached. When Beverly complained about the lack of light, so many lights were installed that one solider commented that he felt like he was in an interrogation room. Fortunately, the commanding officer was soon transferred and the new one was much more sympathetic to the library, installing a proper circulation desk and removing the door meant to keep the men out. At the army hospital, Beverly witnessed babies being born, patients healing, and men dying. "The case that caused the most excitement was an army wife who at dusk had backed into a spinning airplane propeller, which had sliced off three pounds of her buttocks, shattered her elbows, and fractured her skull. Her husband . . . came every afternoon for weeks to read Western stories to her as

Did you know...

Beverly Cleary's alma mater, University of California, Berkeley, is one of the most prestigious universities in the United States. Founded in 1866 from the merger of two colleges, it was the first school in the California state university system and its curriculum was modeled on Harvard and Yale universities. Distinguished alumni include Jack London, author of *Call of the Wild*; actor Gregory Peck; authors Joan Didion and Terry McMillan; NBA All-Star Jason Kidd; Jerry Brown and Pete Wilson, former governors of California; and Earl Warren, former chief justice of the U.S. Supreme Court. Eighteen Berkeley professors have been honored with the Nobel Prize. In 1964, Berkeley students unhappy with the school administration led the Free Speech Movement, considered the birth of student activism in the 1960s.

she lay facedown. Everyone followed her progress with concern, and the staff was proud of its work when she was finally able to walk out of the hospital." [115]

The patients requested best-sellers, and one day a best-selling book written by one of Beverly's classmates at Cal crossed her circulation desk. The book was "a nagging reminder every time it crossed our new circulation desk that I, too, wanted to write—if the war would ever end, and I could find the time." [116]

"NOTHING TO SAY"

When the war ended in 1945, Beverly quit her job and returned to being a housewife. It was "a letdown after the stimulating work in the hospital. War had scattered friends, most of them now married and parents of infants, with little time for writing letters." [117] She turned down a few library positions where the work required little interaction with the public. "I told myself that if I was ever going to write a children's book, now was the time to do it. But when I sat down at my typewriter and stared at the paper I had rolled into it, the typewriter seemed hostile, and the paper remained blank. . . . After years of aspiring, I found I had nothing to say. Maybe it had all been a foolish dream." [118]

After suffering a miscarriage, Beverly returned once more to the Sather Gate Book Shop to revive her spirits. After a fun night at a co-worker's house in Berkeley, Beverly insisted she and Clarence move there. They soon bought a five-room house on the side of a hill, only a few minutes away from Clarence's work. In the new linen closet they discovered a ream of typing paper left by the previous owners. Beverly commented to Clarence that she ought to try writing again. When he encouraged her, she joked, "We don't have any sharp pencils." [119] The next day he brought her a pencil sharpener. Yet Beverly couldn't seem to think of anything to write about. She busied herself with decorating the house, and she became close friends with Hannah, the mother of her coworker and friend, Quail. Hannah, who had been a journalist, became a mentor to Beverly. Beverly admired Quail and Hannah's strong and honest relationship.

One day at Sather Gate Beverly picked up a children's book about a puppy. The puppy's silly dialogue prompted Beverly to realize she could write something better. "What was more, I intended to do it as soon as the Christmas rush was over."[120] Not long after, Beverly and Quail met the children's book editor for a national publisher at a lecture. She asked the editor, Elisabeth Hamilton, if she ever wrote a letter to the authors whose books she turned down. Hamilton replied that she did only if the writer showed talent.

HENRY HUGGINS

On January 2, 1949, Beverly "gathered up my typewriter, freshly sharpened pencils, and the pile of paper and sat down at the kitchen table we had stored in the back bedroom. *Write* and no backing out," she told herself.[121] Yet she remained uncertain of what to say. As she sat at that table, Beverly remembered the nonreading boys in Yakima who wished for books about "kids like us."[122] She realized she ought to write a book that the average child could relate to. Memories sieved through her mind as she pondered what the story should be about. She remembered the boys from her Portland childhood. They enjoyed teasing girls and building scooters to race on, usually with a dog hanging around them. She thought back to a woman she had encountered at Oakland Hospital who had brought her children and their dog to the library. The woman told Beverly that the family had arrived by streetcar, which did not allow dogs except in boxes. It had been pouring rain as the woman and her children tried desperately to find a box for the dog. That story provided Beverly with an idea for her own story.

Beverly also wasn't sure she remembered *how* to write. Trying to remember the instructions teachers had given her over the years did not seem to help. It occurred to her that she had spent many hours telling stories to the children of Yakima. In her mind, she began to tell an audience of children the story she had brewing in her head. Then she wrote the first sentence, "Henry Huggins was in the third grade."[123] In college, she'd read a book suggesting that ideas simply existed in the atmosphere, waiting for someone to grab them. The notion appealed to Beverly. "Where Henry's name came from I do not know. It was just there, waiting to be written, but I do know Henry was inspired by the boys on Hancock Street, who seemed eager to jump onto the page. Hancock Street became Klickitat Street because I had always liked the sound of the name when I lived nearby."[124] She named Henry's dog Spareribs, after the leftover ribs Beverly had in her refrigerator. "Writing without research, bibliography, or footnotes was a pleasure. So was rearranging life."[125]

When Beverly finished "Spareribs and Henry," one of her friends, whom she valued for her honesty, read the story. The woman liked it. Beverly sent it to a publisher who rejected the story but included a very encouraging note. The story had "humor, action, and realism" but a short story couldn't really be used by a book publisher. She recommended that Beverly write a full-length book of short stories or to submit her pieces to magazines.[126] In fact, Beverly already had more ideas about the adventures of Henry Huggins. She thought back to the story she'd written as a teenager about the boy who had accidentally been dyed green and turned it into a story about Henry. She recalled an incident she'd witnessed as a child where a football was accidentally thrown through the window of a moving car, which quickly disappeared with the ball. Other stories about Henry came from real-life incidents in Beverly's life.

Many days Beverly prepared a loaf of bread before she started writing. When the bread was done, she stopped writing for the day. She switched from the typewriter to writing her stories on paper, as the ideas seemed to come easier when she wrote them. She remembered the words of her mother, who always urged her to keep her writing funny and simple. She also thought back to the professor at Cal who told students the proper subject for a story was the universal human experience. As she wrote the stories of Henry and his friend, Beverly realized the characters in the stories were only children, as she was. For variety she decided to give someone a sister. Outside, she heard her neighbor calling to another neighbor whose name was Ramona. She wrote down the name and continued on with the story.

When she finished the book, Beverly decided to send it to Elisabeth Hamilton, the editor who said she responded to writers with talent. Six weeks later, the postman, who knew that Beverly was waiting for a reply, ran to her house with a letter. The book had been accepted. Elisabeth Hamilton asked Beverly to make a few revisions and rewrite the final chapter. Beverly was happy to do so, "in my own blood, if necessary."[127] Hamilton suggested she change the name of the dog to Ribs or Ribsy, which sounded more like a name a boy would give to a dog. So Spareribs became Ribsy, and the book was titled simply *Henry Huggins*. To Beverly's immense pride, it was published in 1950. "After all my years of ambition to write, of aiming both consciously and unconsciously toward writing, I had actually written. I was a real live author."[128] She knew the book would not be her last. "I was confident that a satisfying life of writing lay ahead, that ideas would continue to flow."[129]

The 50th anniversary edition of Cleary's first book, Henry Huggins, *originally published in 1950. The book tells the adventures of Henry, a young boy in Portland who befriends a stray dog, who he names Ribsy. Many of the details of Henry's story came from Cleary's own life and were inspirations for individual chapters in the book. Henry's stories emphasize that he is an average boy from an average neighborhood.*

5

Welcome to the Neighborhood

WHEN SHE SAT down at her typewriter to begin *Henry Huggins*, Beverly had planned to write a book "about the maturing of a sensitive female who wanted to write," much like Beverly herself.[130] Instead, she told the story of Henry Huggins, an earnest young boy in Portland who befriends a stray dog. Like all of Beverly's books, "Henry's life is not high drama: he does not solve mysteries or find himself in life-or-death situations. He does the things that many children do: he gets a dog and a paper route, builds a clubhouse, and makes friends."[131] Details of Henry's story came from Beverly's own

Ramona gets revenge on Ribsy, who had eaten her ice cream cone, by hiding his bone in her lunch box. Ribsy chases Ramona to school and traps her at the top of the jungle gym, Ramona holding the bone and screaming and Ribsy barking furiously at the bottom. Ribsy redeems himself, as he always does, when he helps Henry catch a twenty-nine-pound salmon on a fishing trip.

GROWING UP

Henry, an only child, is rattled by the demanding presence of Ramona. In *Henry and Beezus*, her tantrums prevent Henry from bidding on a bike he wants at a public auction. At the end of *Henry and the Paper Route*, Henry has finally won a coveted paper route. Ramona thwarts his attempts to be a good paperboy in the next book, *Henry and the Clubhouse*, by locking him in his clubhouse so that he nearly misses delivering papers. She then follows him on his route, carrying a smaller version of his delivery bag, which embarrasses Henry. Their adversarial relationship changes one snowy day when Henry rescues Ramona, who is stuck in the snow. "Henry finds himself feeling sorry for Ramona as she stands tired, cold, and pathetic in the deep snow. Seeing her suddenly as the small child she is, Henry finds himself helping her, though he does not want to."[135] A customer writes a letter to the local newspaper praising Henry's efforts, and Henry basks in his father's pride, as well as his newfound empathy for Ramona.

Henry's stories, although funny, emphasize that he is an average boy from an average neighborhood. Beverly was interested in writing about children "as they were, not as they should be in the opinion of adults."[136] His problems, which are always treated with humor, "arise naturally out of things of everyday life."[137] Unlike Ramona, Henry doesn't purposefully cause trouble, although he tries to handle it on his own when it arises. Henry's parents usually stay in the background, only stepping forward when Henry truly needs help: finishing the hunt for nightcrawlers and "support[ing] Henry emotionally when Ribsy is lost."[138]

No matter what problems come his way, "Henry's middle name seems to be perseverance."[139] In *Henry and the Paper Route*, he thinks he's come up with a clever idea for selling a subscription—a free kitten with every subscription. When this fails to work, Henry simply gives all the kittens to the local pet shop. Yet Beverly tried not to overemphasize Henry's growing maturity. She commented, "The definition [of a story] does not include the word 'teach.' Any message conveyed by the story must be implicit in the story."[140] Henry's "determination and sense of responsibility" grow stronger over the course of the series, but they are continually tested by the funny situations he finds himself in. "All these problems may seem small, but they loom large in the average child's life, and they are the kind of problems that every child must solve."[141] When she was growing up, Beverly had wanted "most of all to read about problems children could solve themselves."[142] It's appropriate that Beverly, the descendent of pioneers, would instill her characters with the same "can-do" spirit.

Henry Huggins was an immediate success. The Sather Gate Book Shop sold 500 copies during the Christmas season. One critic stated, "This story . . . is written for boys and girls but we defy anyone under seventy not to chuckle over it." Beverly received letters from children who said they found the book "funny and sad."[143] "[Many] boys write to me. Their most frequent comment is that one of the Henry books . . . was the first book the boy enjoyed reading." [144]

ELLEN AND EMILY

Beverly found she did not lack for story ideas. "My mental pump, having been primed by Henry Huggins, was at work on a story about a girl named Ellen Tebbits who had trouble hiding her woolen underwear at ballet class." [145] *Ellen Tebbits* appeared in the following year, 1951. The new book also had roots in real life. To Beverly's endless humiliation, her mother had forced her wear woolen underwear while growing up. Ellen's friend Austine was based on one of Beverly's best friends. In the book, Ellen becomes best friends with a new girl, Austine, who is also hiding in the closet changing into woolen underwear. The two defend each other against a class bully, ride horses, and share secrets. When Ellen volunteers to bring an enormous beet to school, she ends up staining and tearing her dress, which Austine helpfully tapes. Although the girls ask their mothers to make matching dresses, Austine feels jealous of Ellen's, which is much neater. When Ellen's dress is torn, she blames Austine and the two stop speaking. Their painful separation feels like an eternity while each waits for the other to apologize. When Ellen finds out that it was the class bully who tore her dress, she apologizes to Austine and the two are once more friends.

Friendships are the focus of *Ellen Tebbits*. Ellen, an only child like Henry, isn't concerned with growing up or pets and paper routes. Henry had no secrets. Ellen's concern is making friends and sharing the secret of her woolen underwear. The "complexities of relationships" gives *Ellen*

Tebbits its drama.[146] Beverly doesn't shy away from showing the girls' envy of each other; Austine for Ellen's nicer dress and Ellen for Austine's more carefree household. Beverly captures how devastating even small fights can seem between friends. "The good side of having a best friend, Ellen and Austine realize, means having someone with whom to share embarrassing secrets. . . . But having a best friend means fighting as well as sharing good times; and Beverly's detailing . . . shows how and why things can go wrong."[147]

Reviewers praised *Ellen Tebbits* for its sympathy and humor, and called Ellen "a real girl and her adventures full of zest and interest."[148] Even when Ellen is horrified by her predicaments—struggling in the rain to uproot a beet

Did you know...

Klickitat Street is the neighborhood immortalized in the *Henry Huggins* and *Ramona* books. It is a real street in Portland, Oregon, close to where Beverly Cleary grew up. "I had always liked the sound of the name when I lived nearby," Beverly once commented. When Beverly lived there, the street was a few blocks from the city limits, houses were far apart, and snakes could be seen sunning themselves on warm days. Beverly still visits the neighborhood and has said, "It's really a remarkable neighborhood. It's changed very little since I lived there. It's a very stable place."

or playing a rat in the school play, the incidents are conveyed with humor that doesn't deny the characters sympathy.

It wasn't until a decade later that Beverly created a fully autobiographical tale, *Emily's Runaway Imagination*. Unlike Beverly's other works, which are set in the present or recent past, Emily is a young girl growing up in the 1920s in Pitchfork, Oregon, a fictionally disguised Yamhill. Emily's mother often tells her daughter that her imagination runs away with her, and the story revolves around Emily's solitary, but happy, world. The plot contains many details and stories from Beverly's own young life: Emily's mother opens the town's first library and struggles to raise money while Emily quietly hopes for children's books to read. An intimidating neighbor tells her that she is being sold to an old Chinese neighbor who is returning to China. Emily adores church potluck suppers and her grandparent's general store. Even small details, like Emily's love of her mother's long, dark hair, were true to Beverly's past. Emily, the only child of two farmers, is also left free to explore their farm. Like Beverly's parents, Emily's parents struggle to make the farm profitable. Emily's tale "is rich in the details . . . from judging the temperature of a wood stove by touch to the jostling ride in a Tin Lizzie."[149]

Portland, home to Henry and Ellen, and Pitchfork are ultimately havens where children can play safely and be certain they are loved. Although Beverly's parents sold their farm and moved away, Emily is undisturbed in her world. Portland had its ups and down for Beverly, but the fictional Klickitat Street is a quiet slice of American life with tree-lined streets and well-kept homes. Children play after dark without fear and school is just a short block away. Mothers watch each other's children and a grocery store being built on a vacant lot creates much excitement. Emily's world isn't that different from that of Ellen Tebbits or Ramona Quimby. Beverly's books emphasize that "while the trappings of daily life have changed, the daily problems and emotions of children have not." [150]

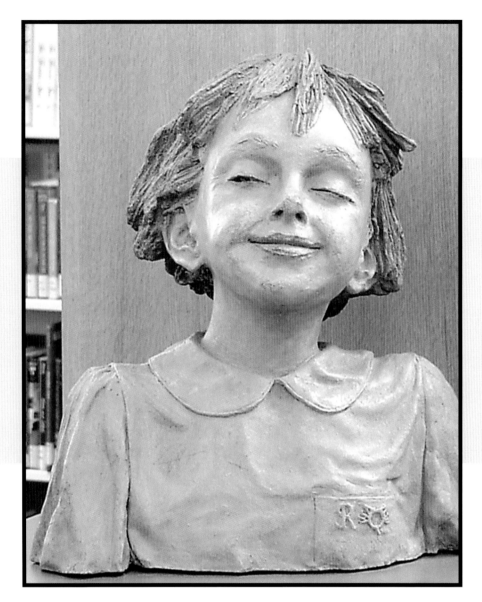

Sculptor Lee Hunt created two busts of Ramona Quimby, one smiling and one scowling, for the Gresham Regional Library in Gresham, Oregon. The plaque of the smiling Ramona features a quote from the book that reads: "'I'm not acting like a pest. I'm singing and skipping,' said Ramona, who had only recently learned to skip with both feet. Ramona did not think she was a pest. No matter what others said, she never thought she was a pest. The people who called her a pest were always bigger and so they could be unfair."

Ramona Forever

EXUBERANT, LOUD, ATTENTION-GRABBING Ramona
Quimby began life as an afterthought in *Henry Huggins*. Realizing that her characters were only children, Beverly slipped in
the character of Ramona, the pesky little sister of Henry's good
friend Beezus. Readers, however, wanted more of the expressive
little girl. A review of *Henry and Ribsy* ended with a request for
an entire book about her. Indeed, Beverly kept thinking about
her "accidental" character. "I hadn't really intended to write so
much about her, but there she was. She kept hanging around and
I kept having Ramona ideas."[151]

Three years later, in 1955, Beverly let Ramona take center stage in *Beezus and Ramona*. The ideas continued and Beverly penned eight more books about Ramona over the next four and a half decades, although Ramona herself only ages from four to nine.

Ramona's adventures have been translated into Japanese, Spanish, Chinese, German, Dutch, French, Danish, and Norwegian. She has endured in Beverly's imagination, as well as in the imagination of children and adults around the world, because of her creativity, high spirits, and outsized personality. Yet it is Ramona's flaws that make her memorable and ultimately lovable. "She gets angry and frustrated, but she struggles to learn the self-control and patience her parents and teachers expect. Her desire for attention and her feelings of embarrassment and confusion cause many readers to iden-tify with her; and her resilience, creativity and pure love of her life make her someone to be admired, even emulated." [152]

THE PEST

Thirteen years passed before Beverly wrote *Ramona the Pest*, the sequel to *Beezus and Ramona*. She was now the mother of twins. Observing their first years of school gave Beverly the inspiration to write about Ramona again. At first she was concerned that children would not want to read about a character younger than themselves or that boys would not want to read a book about a girl. "Gradually I saw that these generalizations did not hold if children found books funny." [153]

She noticed that her twins found "nothing was so funny to them as their memories of kindergarten and nursery school. . . . I began to understand that children would enjoy a book about a younger girl because they would recognize and enjoy feeling superior to their younger selves." [154]

Ramona the Pest begins on Ramona's first day of kindergarten. Her enthusiasm over "the great day" is soon derailed after her teacher, Miss Binney, tells Ramona to find a desk and sit for "the present." Ramona assumes she will receive a present and so she sits and sits, refusing to move until she has received the present. She is crushed when Miss Binney explains that Ramona misunderstood the word "present." "Ramona was so disappointed she had nothing to say. Words were so puzzling. *Present* should mean a present just as *attack* should mean to stick tacks in people."[155]

Kindergarten improves and Ramona takes great delight in learning to print her name, adding a cat tail and whiskers to her Q. However, she can't stop pulling—or boinging—her classmate Susan's thick blond curls. On the exciting day that Ramona loses her first tooth while in school, Miss Binney asks if Ramona can stop pulling Susan's hair. Ramona truthfully says she can't. She is sent home, forgetting her tooth behind. Ramona is devastated—her beloved Miss Binney does not like her. She announces to her parents that she has dropped out of kindergarten. Ramona continues her strike for several more days until Miss Binney sends a note, along with Ramona's tooth, asking Ramona to return. Ramona is thrilled by Miss Binney's note, deciding the teacher must love her after all. She will go back to kindergarten.

Seven years later, in 1975, *Ramona the Brave* appeared. The title is, at first, ironic. The book opens as Ramona, now six years old, is telling her mother how she "defended" Beezus from some older boys who were teasing her. As Beezus tells her side of the story, Ramona is shocked to hear that wiggling her fingers and sticking her tongue out at the boys embarrassed her sister as much as the boys' teasing. For the first time in Ramona's life she sees herself "as Beezus sees her: a nonheroic little girl."[156]

Ramona was used to being considered a little pest, and she knew she sometimes was a pest, but this was something different. She felt as if she were standing aside looking at herself." [157]

Indeed, throughout the book Ramona is often scared or in trouble for bad behavior. After the family builds a spare room for the girls, Ramona is afraid to sleep in the dark alone. At school, the students make owls out of paper bags. Ramona sees Susan copying her project but the teacher sees Susan's owl first and praises her for it. Enraged, Ramona destroys Susan's owl and runs home. But unlike in *Ramona the Pest*, Ramona must continue going to class even though "each of her days seemed to plod among more slowly than the day before." [158] One night she decides she can't continue to be afraid of the dark. Feeling brave, she hides a gorilla book in the living room and goes back to bed. Nothing grabs her and she is safe. The next day, now feeling very brave, she goes a different way to school. On the way Ramona confronts an unleashed German shepherd who growls at her and behaves threateningly. Ramona throws her lunchbox at him and then her shoe and flees to school wearing only one shoe. The school secretary calls her "a very brave girl." [159] This time, Ramona knows it is true.

As the title indicates, Ramona is not the same pest who dropped out of kindergarten. She still works very hard to be the center of attention and reacts rashly when things don't go her way. Yet, as one reviewer put it, she is "semi-reformed . . . a little girl trying hard to grow up, sometimes misunderstanding and misunderstood." [160] During the next several books, Ramona's problems usually center on her mixed-up feelings for the people in her life. She might not always be brave, but she is beginning to face the consequences of her sometimes impulsive behavior in her own inimitable way. Ramona apologizes to Susan in front of the class for ruining Susan's owl, but in private she informs Susan that she is still "a copycat—who stinks!"[161] An artistic, imaginative girl, Ramona doesn't want anyone to take the power of expression away from her.

A HAPPY FAMILY

Beverly's next two books, *Ramona and Her Father* and *Ramona and Her Mother*, were written, she said, "in rebellion against the portrayal of family life in many contemporary children's books."[162] Beverly reminds the reader throughout both books that neither Ramona nor her family is perfect and that being flawed is perfectly acceptable. After all, "I had the same feelings [as Ramona] but I didn't do the same things Ramona does."[163] While Henry Huggins is concerned with the "outer trappings of growing up—getting a bicycle, getting and keeping a paper route—Ramona deals more with inner matters—feeling grownup and getting along with teachers and other children —and with the often-complex relationships between the members of a loving family."[164]

Ramona continues her struggle to grow up with plenty of humor and misunderstandings. *Ramona and Her Father* began with an idea for the last chapter, about Ramona's refusal to be in a Christmas pageant. Beverly has said she typically writes as ideas come to her, not with an entire story in mind. "I usually start with a couple of ideas, not necessarily at the beginning of the book, and I just write."[165] Beverly's next few books, written in the 1970s, reflect certain changes in society—Mrs. Quimby takes a job outside the home, and Beezus and Ramona discuss the possibility of their parents divorcing.

In the latest Ramona chapter, the family must deal with financial stress and pressure when Mr. Quimby loses his job. At first Ramona is very excited to be home with her father, especially since her mother is now working full-time at a doctor's office. Mr. Quimby, however, is too preoccupied to enjoy the time with his younger daughter.

> He could not take her to the park because he had to stay near the telephone. Someone might call to offer him a job. Ramona grew uneasy. Maybe he was too worried to love her anymore.[166]

As the months go by, the entire family seems short-tempered, even their cat, Picky-picky, who eats the Halloween pumpkin instead of his cheap cat food. Beezus challenges her father to quit smoking—putting up signs around the house warning of the dangers of smoking, even slipping rolled-up notes in his cigarette pack. Mr. Quimby decides to quit, which makes him even more irritable. As Christmas nears, Ramona is worried the family won't have any money for gifts and that her mother won't have time to sew a costume for the school pageant. She is even more upset when she catches her father smoking a cigarette. She asks her father why they aren't a happy family.

> For some reason Mr. Quimby smiled. "I have news for you, Ramona," he said. "We *are* a happy family."
>
> "We are?" Ramona was skeptical.
>
> "Yes, we are." Mr. Quimby was positive. "No family is perfect. Get that idea out of your head. And nobody is perfect either. All we can do is work at it. And we do."[167]

At the end of the book, Mr. Quimby finds a job and Ramona accepts an imperfect sheep costume, happy that at least she and her family love each other.

Ramona and Her Father marked a shift away from Ramona as the center of attention to a more complete view of the world around her. "With this work, Cleary begins to focus not just on the child growing up, but on the family. . . . Now, with school not quite as much an adventure Cleary begins to emphasize the Quimby family as a whole, though Ramona is still the focus."[168] Her parents are more fully realized as people, sometimes irritable and worried, while Beezus's rebellious campaign against smoking indicates that she is becoming an adolescent and developing her own sense of self. Ramona begins to worry more—not just imaginary worries like a monster under the bed, but the future of her family. "[Her father] becomes the focus of some of her deepest worries. . . . now Ramona begins to extend her sympathies and empathies to others."[169] This worry repeats itself in *Ramona and Her Mother*, with Beezus and Ramona as the horrified onlookers during a fight between their parents. The girls spend a long, frightened night together, and Ramona wonders whether their parents will divorce. The next morning Mr. and Mrs. Quimby are joking once more, and they tell their surprised daughters that no family is perfect and that even when they sometimes fight, they still love each other.

Life in *Ramona Quimby, Age 8* continues to be full of challenges. Mr. Quimby is now taking college classes, planning to become a teacher. Mrs. Quimby is still working full time. After school Ramona is looked after at her friend Howie's house, where she is pestered by Howie's annoying younger sister, Willa Jean. Ramona's happiness at school is disrupted when she cracks a "hard-boiled" egg on her head that turns out to be uncooked. Her head full of raw egg, Ramona goes to the principal's office to wash it out. There she overhears her beloved teacher call Ramona a "show-off" and "a nuisance." Ramona is devastated and overcome with self-pity. "Her body felt numb and so did her heart.

She could never, never face Mrs. Whaley again. Never."[170] Once more Ramona cannot understand why her teachers don't see the good girl Ramona believes herself to be. Ramona is miserable until she finally asks Mrs. Whaley why she is a nuisance and is overjoyed to discover she has misunderstood her teacher.

One dreary, rainy Sunday, the family is irritable and gloomy until Mr. Quimby decides they need a break and takes the family out to eat. When they try to pay their bill, they discover than an older man who had spoken to Ramona had paid for them. When Beezus remarks that the man's gift was a "happy ending," Ramona corrects her. "A happy ending for today. . . . Tomorrow they would

Did you know...

Klickitat Street and Beverly Cleary were honored in 1995 with the unveiling of the Beverly Cleary Sculpture Garden for Children in Grant Park. Grant Park appears often in Beverly's books, and is where Henry once dug for thousands of nightcrawlers. The garden began as the idea of a group of teachers, librarians, booksellers, and neighbors who decided to create statues of Henry, Ramona, and Ribsy. They put on a play about Ramona and sold a map of the places mentioned in Beverly's books to raise money for the sculpture garden. The garden consists of the statues cast in bronze, a wading pool and fountain, benches, and paving stones featuring book titles and quotes.

begin all over again."[171] Ramona is clearly growing up and recognizing that life isn't about happily ever after and that she must work as hard as her parents and Beezus to make the family get along.

RAMONA'S WORLD

After *Ramona Forever* appeared in 1984, there were no Ramona books until 1999, when *Ramona's World* came out. The new book was greeted happily by old fans. Beverly, then eighty-three years old, hadn't planned to slip into the voice of a nine-year-old. "Ramona just wouldn't let me alone. I would go about my daily business and she kept intruding. Finally she just insisted. She said, 'Come on, sit down and write the book.' So I did."[172]

In *Ramona's World*, Ramona makes her first close female friend, named Daisy. She is grumpy at school because she gets poor grades for spelling and grumpy at home because her baby sister Roberta receives more attention. One of the book's funnier moments comes when Ramona is briefly put in charge of Roberta, who promptly gets her head stuck inside the cat's scratching post. Ramona coaxes Roberta to stop screaming and frees her just before their mother arrives home. At Ramona's tenth birthday party, her old nemesis Susan breaks down in tears, showing Ramona that other people also carry around their own mixed-up feelings: "'I'm supposed to be perfect every single minute,' said Susan, her chin quivering. How awful, thought Ramona, beginning to feel sorry for Susan."[173]

Over the *Ramona* series, Ramona evolves from the center of attention to someone who recognizes that she is somewhat of a role model for her little sister and Willa Jean. She realizes "how hard growing up is and how far she has come."[174]

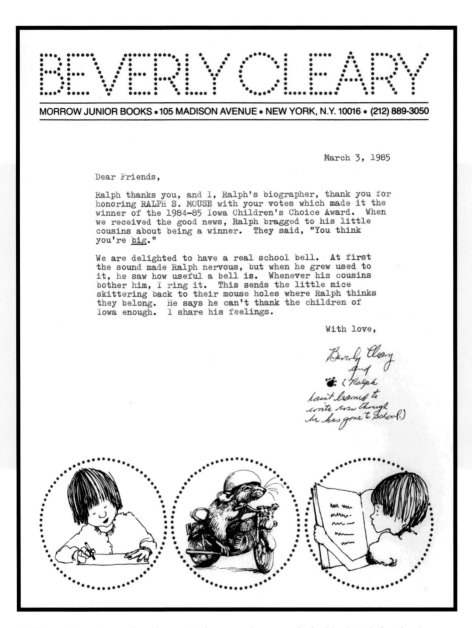

BEVERLY CLEARY

MORROW JUNIOR BOOKS • 105 MADISON AVENUE • NEW YORK, N.Y. 10016 • (212) 889-3050

March 3, 1985

Dear Friends,

Ralph thanks you, and I, Ralph's biographer, thank you for
honoring RALPH S. MOUSE with your votes which made it the
winner of the 1984-85 Iowa Children's Choice Award. When
we received the good news, Ralph bragged to his little
cousins about being a winner. They said, "You think
you're big."

We are delighted to have a real school bell. At first
the sound made Ralph nervous, but when he grew used to
it, he saw how useful a bell is. Whenever his cousins
bother him, I ring it. This sends the little mice
skittering back to their mouse holes where Ralph thinks
they belong. He says he can't thank the children of
Iowa enough. I share his feelings.

With love,

Beverly Cleary
and
🐭 (Ralph
hasn't learned to
write even though
he has gone to school.)

*A letter from Beverly Cleary to her readers, on behalf of Ralph, the hero
of* Ralph S. Mouse, *which was one of the winners of the 1984–1985 Iowa
Children's Choice Award. The award is unusual because it gives children an
opportunity to choose the books that receive the award. Cleary wrote several
books from the point of view of an animal, including* Ribsy, Socks, *and the*
Ralph S. Mouse *series.*

7

Dear Author

FROM HER EARLIEST books, Beverly's young fans have created a unique relationship with their favorite author. She has received scores of letters over the years, at times more than 100 a day. Children write to Beverly about her books and question her closely about the life of an author. But mostly they write about themselves, revealing their innermost thoughts and feelings. Beverly has described these letters as "a constant education." [175]

Beverly herself had thought as a young girl that "authors should stay out of sight." [176] She enjoyed books less when personal details about the author intruded on the page. As such, Beverly didn't always feel comfortable talking to children about her books. "Whenever I have faced an audience of children, I have thought of all this and wondered if I was standing between my books and my readers and why I was not home writing instead of trying to reach an audience that sometimes consisted of as many as 400 children from kindergarten on up."[177] She was surprised to learn that children are always curious about her life.

Each decade brings a different type of letter, Beverly has said. When she first began writing in the 1950s, letters inquired about where she found her ideas or what was her favorite food. Others asked for help in becoming writers themselves. When television brought celebrities into every family's living room, the content of Beverly's fan mail changed. The questions became more sophisticated; readers asked how much money she made and whether she knew other famous people. "Their celebrity-oriented questions have begun to worry me. 'Do you get a lot of publicity?' they ask, 'Have you been on national TV?' 'Are any of your books best sellers?' 'Do you have a limo?'. . . . Children often say they hope I will read their letters and 'not just your secretary (sic)'."[178]

Many of her letters arrive from classrooms, where students have been instructed to write to an author. Such letters usually ask less about books than about Beverly's life. "The questions . . . leave me wondering what an author's favorite ice cream, color or television program has to do with reading; and why children are laboriously writing letters concerned with the trivialities of authors' lives when they could be reading."[179]

Although she can't answer all the letters she receives, Beverly takes care to respond to what she called "from the heart letters."[180] These letters allow her to "keep track not only of readers' responses to her works but of the readers' own concerns."[181] These letters are personal missives from the letter-writer's own life: "[C]hildren who dislike living in mobile homes; a lonely little girl whose father is stationed in the Philippines and who has brought her friends with her in books; a child whose family built a log cabin in the woods and who lives without electricity; children of all races—I know from the pictures they enclose—who write as children, with no mention of color; blind children whose teachers translate their Braille letters; brain-damaged children whose brave letters are barely intelligible; wealthy children who write of horses, swimming pools, and the latest video equipment; . . . inner-city

Did you know...

All of Beverly Cleary's books are illustrated, providing fantastic visual expression of the events and moods of the characters. Over the years, Beverly has worked with a number of illustrators. The first, Louis Darling, paid great attention to detail. In *Ramona the Pest*, Beverly writes about a kindergarten teacher attempting to round up sixty-eight students for a Halloween parade; in the illustration, there are sixty-eight figures drawn. Alan Tiegreen's later illustrations show Ramona as skinny and barely formed. Beverly Cleary's other illustrators include Paul O. Zelinsky for *Dear Mr. Henshaw*, Beatrice Darwin for *Socks*, and Joe and Beth Krush for *Emily's Runaway Imagination*.

children who wish they could live in Henry Huggins's neighborhood . . . happy children, grieving children, exuberant children, sick children."[182] While the details of their lives vary, their "deepest feelings remain the same. . . . They want to be loved by their parents, they want pets, they think their brothers and sisters could be nicer."[183]

"FOR ALL THE BRAVE AND LONELY CHILDREN"

As the decades passed, an increasing number of children wrote to Beverly about their parents' divorce. In 1982, she received letters from "several boys unknown to one another: 'Please write a book about a boy whose parents are divorced'."[184] Wanting to write a different sort of book, one removed from the relatively peaceful world of Klickitat Street, Beverly thought about a book that would somehow address the thousands of letter-writers over the years and in particular those who wrote from the heart. Snippets and details Beverly overheard in her own life found their way into the new book. "An overheard sentence spoken in grief by a strange woman: 'It's so terrible when his father promises to call and doesn't.' A remark by a teacher: 'This kid in my class rigged up a burglar alarm for his lunch box. It made a terrible racket'."[185] She decided to write a book for "all the brave and lonely children I have ever known who have found books and libraries to be their best friends."[186]

From those bare details Beverly wrote *Dear Mr. Henshaw*, the story of Leigh Botts, an only child and aspiring writer whose parents are recently divorced. Rather than narrate Leigh's life, Beverly let him tell his own story. The book is a series of letters between Leigh and Boyd Henshaw, his favorite author, whom Leigh writes to as part of a class assignment. Mr. Henshaw, in return, asks Leigh questions about his own life. After Mr. Henshaw suggests that Leigh start a diary to express his inner thoughts, *Dear Mr. Henshaw* switches to a diary format. Beverly chose to present the book in Leigh's voice because "children who want to write should look within themselves, not within the books of others."[187] His life isn't easy. Leigh is a new boy at a school in California without any friends. He loves his mother and misses his father, a truck driver who is always on the road, and his dog Bandit, who travels with his father. Even his lunch becomes a disappointment when a thief begins stealing the treats his mother leaves for him each day.

Leigh is torn between resenting his father for leaving and sadness. His view of divorce is how a child would see it, confused and angry, wondering if he is to blame. Leigh isn't happy in his new life, living with a hardworking mother in a tiny house, while his dog is with his father on the road. His father rarely calls and when he does he calls Leigh "kid," as if unable to remember his son's name. After a talk with his mother, Leigh begins to understand that the trouble between his parents was longstanding and had nothing to do with Leigh. Leigh befriends the school janitor, who points out to Leigh that everyone has their own problems and it's up to Leigh to think positively.

> "Who wants to be friends with someone who scowls all the time?" asked Mr. Fridley. "So you've got problems. Well, so has everyone else, if you take the trouble to notice." I thought of Dad up in the mountains chaining up eight heavy wheels in the snow, and I thought of Mom squirting deviled crab into hundreds of little cream puff shells and making billions of tiny sandwiches for golfers to gulp down and wondering if Catering by Katy would be able to pay her enough to make rent.[188]

Leigh starts to take responsibility for his own happiness. He writes a story for a class contest about delivering a load of grapes with his father and receives honorable mention. After Leigh rigs a burglar alarm for his lunch, the thefts stop and Leigh makes a new friend. After a visit from his father at the end of the book, Leigh feels "sad and a whole lot better at the same time."[189]

Dear Mr. Henshaw resonated deeply with readers. For the first time Beverly received letters from adults. "Teachers wrote that the book would be valuable for classroom discussion because so many pupils came from single parent homes. Mothers struggling to rear sons without help from fathers wrote moving letters of appreciation."[190] Children wrote letters saying they had read the book over and over. "Another girl said she was *so* glad Leigh's parents didn't get together at the end. Many told me how hard life is in a new school, that their lives were very much like Leigh's, or that there were 'lots of kids like Leigh' in their school."[191] By writing a book about "the kind of emotions that do not change," Beverly created a timeless work.[192] In 1984, the book was awarded the Newbery Medal, an award given by the American Library Association to the author of the most distinguished contribution to American literature for children.

A DOG, A CAT, AND A MOUSE

In 1991, Beverly wrote the sequel to Leigh's life, *Strider*. Strider is the name Leigh and his best friend Barry give a dog they find abandoned on the beach. To keep up with Strider's enormous energy, Leigh begins running with the dog on mornings before school. Leigh evolves into a serious runner and is recruited onto the high school track team. In this book, Strider has taken the place of Bandit.

Pets have always been extremely important in Beverly's books. Both Leigh's and Henry Huggins's lives are changed by their dogs. Taking care of Strider and Ribsy brings them both adventure and a sense of responsibility.

These dogs are as expressive as any human. When Leigh and Barry discover Strider, he is sitting forlornly on the beach, presumably abandoned by his owner. "This dog looked up at me with his ears laid back and the saddest look I have ever seen on a dog's face. If dogs could cry, this dog would be crying hard. . . . The dog wagged his docked tail. It wasn't a happy wag. It was an anxious wag. Dogs can say a lot with their tails."[193]

Over the years Beverly has written several books from the point of view of an animal, including *Ribsy*, *Socks*, and the Ralph S. Mouse series. The books "do not depart from the Cleary tradition: Socks and Ralph struggle with many of the problems their readers do and learn for themselves the pain and loneliness and the triumphs of growing up."[194]

At the beginning of his story, Socks is a very contented cat, "loving, loved, and determined to get his own way."[195] His secure place in the world is turned upside down when his owners, the Brickers, welcome baby Charles into their household. Once the center of attention, Socks is now overlooked and, he believes, unloved. Depressed and unsure about this tiny new creature, Socks eats too much and grows lazy. For a brief time he becomes an outdoor cat, but after being bullied and beaten by a neighborhood tough cat, he goes indoors again, working hard to avoid the baby. Charles, however, tries to befriend Socks, and when he says his first word, it is his name for Socks, "Ticky." In the end, the Brickers recognize that their son enjoys Socks's company and Socks fully becomes a member of the family once more.

Socks's relationship with Charles mirrors how a sibling might feel about the arrival of a younger brother or sister. Yet Socks is portrayed very much as a cat. He lacks the knowledge to understand why Mrs. Bricker's lap grows smaller until her stomach is too large for Socks. He can't understand why he feels the way he does, he just knows that he wants to be loved.

Beverly's son Malcolm's struggles while learning to read provided the inspiration for the first book about Ralph S. Mouse, *The Mouse and the Motorcycle*. Malcolm loved motorcycles, but there were no books for young children on the subject, leading Beverly to write a book that would engage a young boy. Ralph S. Mouse is no less a complicated portrait of an animal, but one who acts with more understanding of the human world. Most importantly, in *The Mouse and the Motorcycle* he can communicate with a boy who stays at the hotel where Ralph and his family live. The two bond over their shared love of motorcycles, which allows them to understand each other. Ralph is a young mouse, eager to play with his new friend's toy motorcycle. His family, however, does not encourage Ralph's independence. Relatives have disappeared after encounters with a maid and a laundry basket, and Ralph's own father was poisoned by an aspirin tablet. The outdoors is even more dangerous, with watchful owls waiting to snatch a mouse up. "Their lives are hemmed in by danger and the powerlessness of the very small; it's no wonder they are as timid as, well, as mice." [196] Yet Ralph does not think of himself as a helpless mouse. Like all children he yearns to explore the world. When he is able to ride the motorcycle at night freely he feels like "a dare-devil now, [riding] in a giddy circle around the ashtray stand. He had a feeling of cockiness he had never known before. Who said mice were timid? Ha!" [197]

The next two books, *Runaway Ralph* and *Ralph S. Mouse*, contrast Ralph's mouse-eye view of the human world with the danger he faces almost constantly in his quest for independence and growth. His view of the world is naïve, but Ralph's efforts to fearlessly be a part of it give "power to the powerless."[198] In both books, he meets young boys who are lonely and looking for excitement, just like him. They act as guardians during Ralph's forays into the human world and are rewarded with deep loyalty from Ralph. The appeal of Beverly's animal characters is that their range of "emotional responses is wide and deep."[199]

Beverly Cleary walking arm in arm with her husband Clarence in London's Kensington Gardens. She and Clarence live in Carmel, California, and she sticks with the same writing routine that she has used for fifty years. When she has an idea for a book, she sits down each day after breakfast and writes longhand with a pen and yellow legal pad.

8

Winning at Growing Up

IN THE FIFTY years since Beverly Cleary sat down at a typewriter and commanded herself to write, she has created a body of children's literature that is without equal. Her goals as a writer, though, were modest. Shortly after *Henry Huggins* was published, as she contemplated what lay ahead, Beverly made two resolutions: "I would ignore all trends and I would not let money influence any decisions I would make about my books"[200]

Today, Beverly lives with her husband Clarence in Carmel, California, and has much the same writing routine as she did five decades ago. She begins each book with a handful of ideas. When an idea won't leave her alone, she sits each day after breakfast and writes longhand with a pen and yellow legal pad. "I think about a book long before I begin to write. . . . I don't begin with Page 1. If I have characters vividly in mind, and several incidents, I just write."[201]

She is flexible with her expectations. "Some parts of my stories come out right the first time; others I rewrite several times. . . . If I start a book and do not like it, I just don't finish it."[202] For her, writing remains a pleasure and she doesn't plan where the story or will go or how it will turn out. "I revise until a little light bulb clicks off and I know it's done."[203]

Beverly's gift for creating realistic, unsentimental characters comes from her imagination infused with careful

Did you know...

Beverly Cleary has also written several picture books for toddlers. *Hullabaloo ABC* is an alphabet book written in rhyme that follows the adventures of a boy and girl exploring a farm similar to where Beverly grew up. *The Real Hole* is the first in Beverly's series about twins Jimmy and Janet, followed by *Two Dog Biscuits, The Growing Up Feet,* and *Janet's Thingamajigs.* A new Jimmy and Janet story is due in 2005. *Lucky Chuck* follows Chuck as he takes care of his motorcycle and learns to ride safely. *Petey's Bedtime Story* is about the fantastic stories Petey likes to tell at bedtime.

observance of everyday life. She has said, "My writing is a collaboration between my adult self and my child self. We both have to be pleased."[204] With extensive editing and rewrites, the entire process to complete a book takes six months. She has long had the habit of starting a book on January 2, the day she began *Henry Huggins*.

Beverly's writing career has been extremely prolific. Besides the books for children in elementary and middle school, she has created pictures books and simpler stories for toddlers, a series of novels for teenagers that deal with romance, plays, television scripts, and two autobiographies, *A Girl From Yamhill* and *My Own Two Feet*. She is also one of the most widely honored children's writers. Beverly has been honored with nearly every award a children's author can receive. Besides receiving the Newbery Medal for *Dear Mr. Henshaw*, Beverly's books *Ramona and Her Father* and *Ramona Quimby, Age 8* were both named Newbery Honor books. *Ramona Quimby, Age 8*; *Ramona and Her Father*; and the Ralph S. Mouse series are all among the best-selling children's books of all time.[205] An award called the Beverly Cleary Children's Choice Award for children's books has been established in her name by the Oregon Educational Media Association (OEMA), and in late 2003, Beverly received the highest award given to an artist by the United States government, the National Medal of the Arts.

Yet her greatest reward is the children who continue to reap pleasure from her books. "Reading made a great difference in quality of my childhood," she has said. "I'm happy to learn that my books do the same for children today."[206] Readers who are now adults affectionately remember their fondness for Ramona, Ellen Tebbits, Henry Huggins, and Leigh Botts. One fan has written, "What

On November 13, 2003, Beverly Cleary (center) received the National Medal of the Arts, the highest award given to an artist by the United States government. She is shown posing with President Bush and (from the left) blues musician Buddy Guy, dancer Suzanne Farrell, actor and director Ron Howard, and Mac Christensen, president of the Mormon Tabernacle Choir.

causes a California child who has never seen or heard of long underwear to so readily empathize with poor Ellen? . . . It is because the feelings are so genuine."[207]

It is Beverly's belief that children are interested in the ordinary and in characters that remind them of themselves that ensures her books will remain popular for generations to come. Serious subjects are handled with sympathy and humor. The books Beverly read as a child depicted children in an idealized, "goody-two shoes" way, but her own books have contributed greatly to a children's literature that reflects a more natural version of childhood where actual problems can be addressed. Her characters are nuanced and constantly changing. As Ramona tells herself at the end of *Ramona Forever*, she is "winning at growing up."[208] The "pioneer spirit" that Beverly's parents impressed upon her as a child lives on through her characters, who work hard at being themselves.

1. Cleary, Beverly. *The Girl from Yamhill*, New York, NY: Avon Books, 1988, 95.

2. Berg, Julie. *Beverly Cleary*, Minneapolis, MN: Abdo & Daughters, 1993, 9.

3. Kelly, Joanne. *The Beverly Cleary Handbook*, Englewood, CO: Teacher Ideas Press, 1996, 2.

4. *A Girl from Yamhill*, 99.

5. Ibid., 101.

6. Ibid., 102.

7. Ibid., 103.

8. Ibid., 103.

9. Ibid., 108.

10. Ibid., 117–18.

11. Ibid., 118.

12. Berg, *Beverly Cleary*, 12.

13. Van Allsburg, Chris. "Waxing Creative." *Publishers Weekly*. July 17, 1995.

14. *A Girl from Yamhill*, 118.

15. *The Beverly Cleary Handbook*, 3.

16. *A Girl from Yamhill*, 118.

17. Pflieger, Pat. *Beverly Cleary*, Boston, MA: Twayne Publishers, 1991, 1.

18. World of Beverly Cleary, *www.beverlycleary.com*.

19. Pflieger, *Beverly Cleary*, 18.

20. Ibid., 17.

21. Smith, Barbara. "Beverly Cleary's Childhood Memories Make Great Children's Stories." Third Floor Publishing, *www.chfweb.com/ smith/bcleary.html*.

22. Cleary, Beverly. *My Own Two Feet*, New York: NY: Avon Books, 1995, 236.

23. Ibid., 236.

24. Pflieger, *Beverly Cleary*, 12.

25. Ibid., 184.

26. *A Girl from Yamhill*, 10.

27. Ibid., 12.

28. Ibid., 16.

29. Ibid., 21.

30. Ibid., 23.

31. Ibid., 5.

32. Ibid., 9.

33. Ibid., 10.

34. Ibid., 42.

35. Ibid., 24.

36. Ibid., 26.

37. Pflieger, *Beverly Cleary*, 2.

38. *A Girl from Yamhill*, 65.

39. Ibid., 65.

40. Pflieger, *Beverly Cleary*, 3.

41. *A Girl from Yamhill*, 69.

42. Ibid., 70.

43. Ibid., 71.

44. Ibid., 71.

45. Ibid., 93.

46. Ibid., 96.

47. Pflieger, *Beverly Cleary*, 5.

48. *A Girl from Yamhill*, 22.

49. Ibid., 131.

50. Ibid., 132.

51. Ibid., 140.

52. Ibid., 141.

53. Ibid., 141.

54. Ibid., 142.

55. Ibid., 152.

56. Ibid., 154.

57. Ibid., 178.

58. Ibid., 178.

59. Ibid., 179.

60. Ibid., 179.

61. Ibid., 194–198.
62. Ibid., 199.
63. Ibid., 200.
64. Ibid., 207.
65. Ibid., 218.
66. Ibid., 219.
67. Ibid., 257.
68. Ibid., 272.
69. Ibid., 288.
70. Ibid., 344.
71. Ibid., 341.
72. *My Own Two Feet*, 9.
73. Ibid., 14.
74. Ibid., 20.
75. Ibid., 26.
76. Ibid., 32.
77. Ibid., 39.
78. Ibid., 51.
79. Ibid., 57.
80. Ibid., 61.
81. Ibid., 65.
82. Ibid., 96.
83. Ibid., 103.
84. Ibid., 103.
85. Ibid., 114.
86. Ibid., 115.
87. Ibid., 117.
88. Ibid., 118.
89. Ibid., 120–121.
90. Ibid., 125.
91. Ibid., 134.
92. Ibid., 138.
93. Ibid., 151.
94. Ibid., 184.
95. Ibid., 188.
96. Ibid., 191.
97. Ibid., 206.
98. Ibid., 215.
99. Ibid., 210.
100. Ibid., 211.
101. Ibid., 214.
102. Ibid., 222.
103. Ibid., 223.
104. Ibid., 224.
105. Ibid., 226.
106. Ibid., 229.
107. Ibid., 230.
108. Ibid., 234–235.
109. Ibid., 236.
110. Ibid., 236–37.
111. Ibid., 238.
112. Ibid., 247.
113. Ibid., 277.
114. Ibid., 290.
115. Ibid., 300.
116. Ibid., 305.
117. Ibid., 320.
118. Ibid., 321.
119. Ibid., 325.
120. Ibid., 328.
121. Ibid., 329.
122. Ibid., 330.
123. Ibid., 332.
124. Ibid., 332.
125. Ibid., 333.
126. Ibid., 334.
127. Ibid., 341.
128. Ibid., 344.
129. Ibid., 345.
130. Pflieger, *Beverly Cleary*, 20.
131. Ibid., 43.

132. Ibid., 46.

133. Cleary, Beverly. *Henry Huggins*, New York, NY: Dell Publishing, 1950, 28.

134. Pflieger, *Beverly Cleary*, 25.

135. Ibid., 37.

136. Ibid., 14.

137. Ibid., 22.

138. Ibid., 43.

139. Ibid., 23.

140. Ibid., 16.

141. Ibid., 45.

142. Ibid., 45.

143. Ibid., 24.

144. Ibid., 42.

145. *My Own Two Feet*, 345.

146. Pflieger, *Beverly Cleary*, 111.

147. Ibid., 112.

148. Ibid., 94.

149. Ibid., 116.

150. Ibid., 109.

151. World of Beverly Cleary, *www.beverlycleary.com/teaching/talkingwith.html*.

152. World of Beverly Cleary, *www.beverlycleary.com/teaching/index.html*.

153. Pflieger, *Beverly Cleary*, 55.

154. Ibid., 55.

155. Cleary, Beverly. *Ramona the Pest*, New York, NY: Dell Publishing, 1968, 19.

156. Pflieger, *Beverly Cleary*, 60.

157. Cleary, Beverly. *Ramona the Brave*, New York, NY: Avon Books, 1975, 19.

158. Ibid., 120.

159. Ibid., 189.

160. Pflieger, *Beverly Cleary*, 61.

161. *Ramona the Brave*, 117.

162. Pflieger, *Beverly Cleary*, 69.

163. Herron, Celia. "Cleary Thinks Books Should Be Fun." *Christian Science Monitor*, May 14, 1982.

164. Pflieger, *Beverly Cleary*, 50.

165. World of Beverly Cleary, *www.beverlycleary.com/teaching/talkingwith.html*.

166. Cleary, Beverly. *Ramona and Her Father*, New York, NY: Dell Publishing, 1975, 33.

167. Ibid., 158.

168. Pflieger, *Beverly Cleary*, 66.

169. Ibid., 67.

170. Cleary, Beverly. *Ramona Quimby, Age 8*, New York, NY: Dell Publishing, 1981, 69.

171. Ibid., 190.

172. Nieves, Evelyn. "On Klickitat Street, Beverly Cleary is Forever Ramona." *New York Times*. December 1, 1999.

173. Cleary, Beverly. *Ramona's World*, New York, NY: HarperCollins, 1999, 186.

174. Pflieger, *Beverly Cleary*, 185.

175. "After Forty Years, Kid-Lit Queen Beverly Cleary's Gentle Tales Are Turning Up on Television." *People Weekly*, October 3, 1988.

176. Cleary, Beverly. "Why Are Children Writing to Me Instead of Reading?" *New York Times*, November 10, 1985.

177. Ibid.

178. Ibid.

179. Ibid.

180. Frederick, Heather Vogel. "Beverly Cleary." *Publishers Weekly*, November 22, 1999.

181. Pflieger, *Beverly Cleary*, 143.

182. Ibid., 144–145.

183. Ibid., 145.

184. Ibid., 145.

185. Ibid., 146.

186. Ibid., 152.

187. Ibid., 146.

188. Cleary, Beverly. *Dear Mr. Henshaw*, New York, NY: William Morrow and Company, 1983, 80–81.

189. Ibid., 134.

190. Pflieger, *Beverly Cleary*, 151.

191. Ibid., 152.

192. Ibid., 153.

193. Cleary, Beverly. *Strider*, New York, NY: HarperCollins, 1991, 9.

194. Pflieger, *Beverly Cleary*, 119.

195. Ibid., 132.

196. Ibid., 123.

197. Cleary, Beverly. *The Mouse and the Motorcycle,* New York, NY: HarperCollins, 1965, 56.

198. Pflieger, *Beverly Cleary*, 123.

199. Ibid., 132.

200. *My Own Two Feet*, 346.

201. Herron, "Cleary Thinks Books Should Be Fun," *Christian Science Monitor*, May 14, 1982.

202. Hopkins, Lee Bennett. "Times of Their Lives: Nine Authors and Illustrators Look Back on Significant Chapters from Their Illustrious Careers." *Publishers Weekly*, February 20, 1995.

203. World of Beverly Cleary, *www.beverlycleary.com/teaching/talkingwith.html*.

204. Herron, "Cleary Thinks Books Should Be Fun."

205. Britton, Jason. "All-Time Bestselling Children's Books." *Publishers Weekly*, December 17, 2001.

206. "After Forty Years, Kid-Lit Queen Beverly Cleary's Gentle Tales Are Turning Up on Television." *People Weekly*, October 3, 1988.

207. Chatton, Barbara. "Ramona and Her Neighbors: Why We Love Them." *The Horn Book Magazine*, May 1, 1995.

208. Cleary, Beverly. *Ramona Forever*, New York, NY: HarperCollins, 1984, 182.

1916　Beverly Bunn born to Chester and Mabel Bunn in McMinnville, Oregon, on April 14.

1922　Beverly and her parents move from her hometown, Yamhill, to Portland, Oregon.

1928　Beverly is told by a teacher that she should write children's books when she grows up. Beverly decides she will become a librarian to support herself.

1934　Beverly leaves Portland to attend junior college in California.

1938　Beverly earns a Bachelor's degree in English from the University of California at Berkeley. While attending school, she meets Clarence Cleary, and they fall in love.

1939　Beverly earns a degree in librarianship from the University of Washington. She accepts a librarian position in Yakima, Washington; here she meets children who ask her for books about children like themselves.

1940　Beverly marries Clarence and they move to California.

1941　Beverly works as a sales person at the Sather Gate Book Shop in Berkeley, renowned for its children's books. Through the people she meets at the store, she feels encouraged to write.

1942–1945　Beverly works as a librarian for the army during World War II.

1949　On January 2 Beverly begins writing what will become *Henry Huggins*.

1950　Beverly publishes *Henry Huggins*.

1954　Beverly wins her first award, from the Pacific Northwest Library Association.

1955　Beverly gives birth to twins, Malcolm and Marianne. Publishes *Beezus and Ramona*, the first in the Ramona series.

1983　Beverly wins the Newbery Medal for *Dear Mr. Henshaw*, the highest honor given to a children's author.

2003　Beverly is honored by the president with the National Medal of the Arts award, the highest honor given to an artist in the United States.

HENRY HUGGINS

Third-grader Henry Huggins befriends a stray mutt named Ribsy, who turns his world upside down. Ribsy leads his new owner through a series of adventures, including accidentally knocking a can of green paint on Henry's head. Henry's attempts to earn money for a new football are also a source of amusement.

RAMONA THE PEST

Irrepressible Ramona Quimby is entering kindergarten. She wants to impress her beloved teacher and show how smart she is, but she can't help getting herself in trouble. When she can't stop pulling a classmate's beautiful curls, Ramona refuses to return to kindergarten. Her teacher sends her a letter asking her to come back and Ramona is overjoyed.

RAMONA AND HER FATHER

Ramona's father loses his job, and stress mounts in the Quimby household. Her sister Beezus campaigns to get Mr. Quimby to stop smoking. Ramona fears her father is too worried about finding a job to love her. Mr. Quimby eventually finds a job and Ramona decides she doesn't mind wearing a silly costume in the school Christmas pageant.

RAMONA QUIMBY, AGE 8

Ramona, now a third-grader, is excited to be attending a new school and making a new friend, Danny. She is embarrassed after accidentally cracking a raw egg over her head. She believes her teacher doesn't like her, but finds out it was a misunderstanding. One gloomy Sunday, her father takes the family out for dinner, where they meet an old man who pays for their dinner. Ramona feels lucky to be part of a nice family.

RAMONA FOREVER

Big changes in the Quimby household as Ramona's beloved Aunt Bea prepares to marry Ramona's friend Howie's Uncle Hobart, and Ramona's mother is pregnant. Ramona and Beezus get permission to watch each other alone after school, but their sisterly bond is strained until the afternoon when they discover their cat, Picky-picky, has died. They bury him together and the tension dissolves. When Roberta Quimby finally arrives, Ramona realizes that she is growing up and that Roberta will need Ramona's help, too.

THE MOUSE AND THE MOTORCYCLE

Ralph the mouse lives in an ordinary life in a hotel with his family. He befriends a young boy and discovers they can communicate through their shared love of motorcycles. After his friend falls ill, Ralph risks his life to bring him an aspirin. As thanks, the boy gives Ralph a toy motorcycle to ride.

RUNAWAY RALPH

Ralph is eager to discover the outside world and escape his annoying relatives so he runs away to a nearby summer camp. He is discovered by a boy who keeps Ralph as a pet. When the boy is blamed for stealing a watch that Ralph knows the mean camp cat took, he conspires to return it. After the boy's name is cleared, he returns Ralph and his motorcycle to the hotel.

RALPH S. MOUSE

Ralph is being pressured by his relatives to share the motorcycle, which Ralph resents. A boy living at the hotel takes Ralph to school, and at first Ralph is happy with the attention. The students name him Ralph S. Mouse, the S standing for smart. After Ralph is forced to travel a confusing maze as part of a school project, he wants to go home. With the help of another boy, Ralph escapes the school. His friends give him a mouse-sized sports car, which Ralph is able to share with his relatives.

DEAR MR. HENSHAW

Sixth-grader Leigh Botts writes to his favorite author, Boyd Henshaw, as part of a class assignment. At Henshaw's suggestion, Leigh keeps a diary recording his confusion over his parent's divorce and how he misses his father, a truck driver, and their dog. After making a burglar alarm for his lunch, Leigh makes a new friend. He receives honorable mention in a writing contest and realizes he can accept that he was not responsible for his parent's divorce.

NOVELS

1950 *Henry Huggins*

1951 *Ellen Tebbits*

1952 *Henry and Beezus*

1953 *Otis Spofford*

1954 *Henry and Ribsy*

1955 *Beezus and Ramona*

1956 *Fifteen*

1957 *Henry and the Paper Route*

1958 *The Luckiest Girl*

1959 *Jean and Johnny*

1961 *Emily's Runaway Imagination*

1962 *Henry and the Clubhouse*

1963 *Sister of the Bride*

1964 *Ribsy*

1965 *The Mouse and the Motorcycle*

1967 *Mitch and Amy*

1968 *Ramona the Pest*

1970 *Runaway Ralph*

1973 *Socks*

1975 *Ramona the Brave* and *Ramona and Her Father*

1979 *Ramona and Her Mother*

1981 *Ramona Quimby, Age 8*

1982 *Ralph S. Mouse*

1983 *Dear Mr. Henshaw*

1984 *Ramona Forever*

1988 *A Girl From Yamhill*

1990 *Muggie Maggie*

1991 *Strider*

1995 *My Own Two Feet*

1999 *Ramona's World*

FOR YOUNG READERS

1960   *The Hullabaloo ABC*

1961   *Two Dog Biscuits*

1984   *Lucky Chuck*

1987   *The Growing Up Feet*, *Janet's Thingamajibs*, and *The Real Hole*

1993   *Petey's Bedtime Story*

ANTHOLOGIES

1998   *It's Fine to be Nine*

2000   *It's Fun to be Five*, *It's Heaven to be Seven*, and *It's Great to be Eight*

HENRY HUGGINS

Henry Huggins is an earnest young boy, responsible but interested in proving his independence. His best friend is a dog named Ribsy, whose curiosity leads Henry into adventures he might otherwise avoid. Henry wants to earn his own money, and his attempts to do so often end humorously. He is irritated by Ramona's constant attentions, but comes to realize that she is just a little girl who looks up to him.

RAMONA QUIMBY

Ramona Quimby is known to others as a pest and a show-off, but she believes she is a brave, nice little girl. She's artistic and loves to draw whiskers and a tail on the Q in her name like a cat. She's loud and exuberant, and eager to impress her parents and teachers. As she grows up, she decides she must work harder at getting along with people.

RALPH S. MOUSE

Ralph S. Mouseis too young to be treated as an adult, but too old to play with his younger cousins. He investigates the hotel he lives in and meets young boys whom he can often communicate with. They help him explore the outside world, and he is loyal and helpful in return. He loves motorcycles and toy cars, and feels happiest traveling through the hotel at high speed.

LEIGH BOTTS

Leigh Botts refers to himself as a "medium" boy, unlikely to get anyone's attention. He is in the sixth grade in a new school after his parent's divorce, unsure of where he fits in. He keeps a diary, in which he records his complex feelings toward his mother and father, a truck driver. He realizes that his father is not a perfect man, perhaps more in love with his truck than with a family. Leigh makes a new friend after rigging a burglar alarm for his lunch and wins honorable mention in a writing contest. He decides he might not be entirely "medium" after all.

Beverly Cleary has been honored with nearly every award a children's author can receive. She was first honored in 1954 for *Henry and Ribsy* and has since received an award for nearly every book she has written. In 1983, Beverly received her highest honor to date, the Newbery Medal, for *Dear Mr. Henshaw*. The Newbery Medal is given to the author of the most distinguished contribution to American literature for children. She was named a "living legend" by the Library of Congress in 2000. In 2003, Beverly received the greatest honor bestowed an American artist, the National Medal of the Arts.

"After Forty Years, Kid-Lit Queen Beverly Cleary's Gentle Tales Are Turning Up on Television." *People Weekly*, October 3, 1988.

Berg, Julie. *Beverly Cleary*, Minneapolis, MN: Abdo & Daughters, 1993.

Britton, Jason. "All-Time Bestselling Children's Books." *Publishers Weekly*, December 17, 2001.

Chatton, Barbara. "Ramona and Her Neighbors: Why We Love Them." *The Horn Book Magazine*, May 1, 1995.

Cleary, Beverly. *Dear Mr. Henshaw*, New York, NY: William Morrow and Company, 1983.

Cleary, Beverly. *Henry Huggins*, New York, NY: Dell Publishing, 1950.

Cleary, Beverly. *My Own Two Feet*, New York: NY: Avon Books, 1995.

Cleary, Beverly. *Ramona and Her Father*, New York, NY: Dell Publishing, 1975.

Cleary, Beverly. *Ramona Forever*, New York, NY: HarperCollins, 1984.

Cleary, Beverly. *Ramona Quimby, Age 8*, New York, NY: Dell Publishing, 1981.

Cleary, Beverly. *Ramona's World*, New York, NY: HarperCollins, 1999.

Cleary, Beverly. *Ramona the Pest*, New York, NY: Dell Publishing, 1968.

Cleary, Beverly. *Ramona the Brave*, New York, NY: Avon Books, 1975.

Cleary, Beverly. *Strider*, New York, NY: HarperCollins, 1991.

Cleary, Beverly. *A Girl from Yamhill*, New York, NY: Avon Books, 1988.

Cleary, Beverly. *The Mouse and the Motorcycle*, New York, NY: HarperCollins, 1965.

Cleary, Beverly. "Why Are Children Writing to Me Instead of Reading?" *New York Times*. November 10, 1985.

Frederick, Heather Vogel. "Beverly Cleary." *Publishers Weekly*, November 22, 1999.

Herron, Celia. "Cleary Thinks Books Should Be Fun." *Christian Science Monitor*, May 14, 1982.

Hopkins, Lee Bennett. "Times of Their Lives: Nine Authors and Illustrators Look Back on Significant Chapters from Their Illustrious Careers." *Publishers Weekly*, February 20, 1995.

Kelly, Joanne. *The Beverly Cleary Handbook*, Englewood, CO: Teacher Ideas Press, 1996.

Nieves, Evelyn. "On Klickitat Street, Beverly Cleary is Forever Ramona." *New York Times*, December 1, 1999.

Pflieger, Pat. *Beverly Cleary*, Boston, MA: Twayne Publishers, 1991.

Smith, Barbara. "Beverly Cleary's Childhood Memories Make Great Children's Stories." Third Floor Publishing, *www.chfweb.com/smith/bcleary.html*.

Van Allsburg, Chris. "Waxing Creative." *Publishers Weekly.* July 17, 1995.

World of Beverly Cleary, *www.beverlycleary.com*.

Chatton, Barbara. "Ramona and Her Neighbors: Why We Love Them." *Horn Book* 71 (May/June 1995): 297–304.

Cleary, Beverly. "1980 Regina Recipient (Acceptance Speech)." *Catholic Library World* 52 (July 1980) 22–26.

Cleary, Beverly. "Low Man in the Reading Circle, or, A Blackbird Takes Wing," *Horn Book* 45 (1969): 287.

Cleary, Beverly. "How Long Does It Take to Write a Book?" *Oklahoma Librarian* 21 (July 1971): 14–17.

Cleary, Beverly. "On Talking Back to Authors." *Claremont Reading Conference Yearbook* (1970): 1–11.

Cleary, Beverly. "The Laughter of Children." *Horn Book* 58 (October 1982): 555–64.

Clearly, Beverly. "Newbery Medal Acceptance," *Horn Book* 60 (1984): 431.

Cleary, Beverly. "Writing Books about Henry Huggins," *Top of the News* (December 1957): 11.

Cooper, Ilene. "The Booklist Interview." *Booklist* 87 (1990): 448–49.

Lewis, Claudia. "Beverly Cleary," in *Twentiety-Century Children's Writers*, ed. D.L. Kirkpatrick. New York: St. Martin's Press, 1983.

Malkey, Margaret. "Ramona the Chronotype: The Young Reader and Social Theories of Narrative." *Children's Literature in Education* 22 (June 1991): 97–110.

Reuther, David. "Beverly Cleary," *Horn Book* 60 (1984): 439–43.

Zarrille, James. "Beverly Cleary, Ramona Quimby and the Teaching of Reading." *Children's Literature Association Quarterly* 12 (1988): 131–135.

www.beverlycleary.com
   [The World of Beverly Cleary]

http://falcon.jmu.edu/~ramseyil/cleary.htm
   [Beverly Cleary: Teacher Resource File]

www.trelease-on-reading.com/cleary.html
   [Author Profile: Beverly Cleary]

www.kidsreads.com/authors/au-cleary-beverly.asp
   [Kids Read: Beverly Cleary]

JENNIFER PELTAK grew up in northern Virginia. She received a journalism degree from Temple University and currently resides in Washington, D.C. She is also an avid reader and loved the *Ramona* books as a child.